ALL ABOARD
for CHRISTMAS

ALL ABOARD *for* CHR

ISTMAS

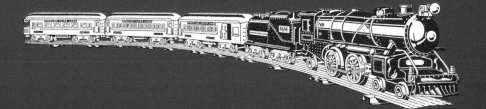

CHRISTOPHER JENNISON

Harry N. Abrams, Inc., Publishers

★

Pages 6–7: A Pullman Company ad featuring a railroad improvisation of "Twas the Night Before Christmas" was seen in the issue of the *Saturday Evening Post* dated December 7, 1946.

Project Manager: CHRISTOPHER SWEET
Editor: SIGI NACSON
Designer: MARY JANE CALLISTER
Production Manager: JUSTINE KEEFE

Library of Congress Cataloging-in-Publication Data

Jennison, Christopher, 1938-
    All aboard for Christmas / Christopher Jennison.
      p. cm.
Includes bibliographical references and index.
    ISBN 0-8109-5614-4 (hardcover)
    1. Railroads—United States—History. 2. Christmas—United States.
3. Voyages and travels. I. Title.
    TF23.J46 2004
    385'.0973—dc22

                       2004005407

Printed and bound in China

10 9 8 7 6 5 4 3 2 1

 Harry N. Abrams, Inc.
100 Fifth Avenue
New York, N.Y. 10011
www.abramsbooks.com

Abrams is a subsidiary of

LA MARTINIÈRE

ACKNOWLEDGMENTS

It's very satisfying to acknowledge in print the many friends and professionals who helped me through every stage of this book's development. First, thanks and much love to Nancy, my wife and best friend, who never lost faith in the book. Bill Purdom had many enthusiastic suggestions to offer, as well as some terrific pictures. Ray Robinson, my co-author of two books, encouraged me throughout the writing process, especially during the sometimes vexing final stages. John Stover was a generous source of information and good advice, and Michael Zega let me borrow several pictures from his indispensable collection.

The following artists, photographers, and writers kindly made their work available to me: Jim Shaughnessey, Gil Reid, Ron Flanary, Ron Hatch, Douglas C. Hart, and Jamie Stringfellow. Additionally, the following helped me track down rights-holders: Steve McShane of the Calumet (Indiana) Regional Archives, Steve Wohlford of Barton-Cotton, Inc., Edward Orloff of The Wylie Agency, Dawn Astram of the Greenwich Workshop, Sharon Berburg at Masterfile, and Eileen Drelick of American Premier Underwriters.

The work of O. Winston Link, Howard Fogg, and Ted Rose was made available by Salem Tamer, Trustee of the O. Winston Link Trust, Margot Fogg, and Polly Rose. It's impossible to imagine an illustrated railroad book without the work of these artists.

Permissions searches are often beset with stumbles, but thanks to the following, requests for this book were secured with a minimum of frustration: Leigh Montville at Condé Nast, Phyllis Carstens of Carstens Publishing Company, Ronald Hussey at Houghton Mifflin, Nat Benchley, Lydia Zelaya at Simon & Schuster, Hal Miller at Kalmbach Publishing, John Rockwell of the Norman Rockwell Family Agency, LLC, Shirley Springman at Curtis Publishing, Elizabeth Ehrensing of The Coca-Cola Company, Cara Lynn Orchard of Lionel L.L.C., the owners of the Lionel and American Flyer images herein, and Robert Ravas at Scott, Foresman, a former publishing colleague.

This is the third book I've written under the guidance of Christopher Sweet, Senior Editor at Abrams. During each assignment he has skillfully and sensitively interceded when necessary, and left me alone when that was necessary. His colleague Sigi Nacson managed the devilish details with admirable patience and tact. Mary Jane Callister, the book's designer, deserves a deep bow for a splendid achievement, in keeping with the high standards that Harry N. Abrams, Inc. routinely sets for itself.

In loving memory of my mother Emily, who took me for rides on *The Green Mountain Flyer*

PREFACE

When we were children it always snowed on Christmas, trains were always on time, and at the end of our holiday journeys grandparents always welcomed us with smothering hugs and piles of presents. If such memories depend largely on our imagination, then it is still essential to preserve them. Imagination lends color and substance to memories of childhood. "Memory is its own vision," wrote the contemporary poet Geoffrey Hill.

Few memories are more enduring than childhood Christmases and train rides. Not so long ago it was routine to board a train at Christmas time. The journey might take a few hours, or consume days and nights of restless anticipation. Reclining chairs and berths cradled weary children lulled to sleep by the gentle rocking of the car and the sounds of whistles and steel wheels. Those fortunate enough to occupy roomettes or bedrooms discovered beds that swung out of the wall, drop-down sinks, mirrors, closets, night lights, shoe compartments, and other mysteries and surprises, all presided over by dignified and seemingly tireless Pullman porters. No endless lines or invasive security measures marred our childhood travels. Holiday crowds were abided happily; they only nourished our excitement. The only discomfort recalled was the agony of "when will we get there, when will we get there?"

The American novelist Willa Cather wrote that there are only two or three great human stories; one of which is the journey. As much as anything else, journeys have characterized the American experience. Journeys to America, of exploration and settlement, and to fulfill personal destinies are principal themes in the American chronicle. Journeys home for Christmas, while less momentous, were, and still are, defining passages. A character in David Baldacci's 2002 best-seller, *The Christmas Train*, described one aspect of the affinity between trains and Christmas by saying, "It's been my experience that most folks who ride trains could care less where they're going. For them it's the journey itself and the people they meet along the way. You see, at every stop this train makes, a little bit of America, a little bit of your country gets on and says hello. That's why trains are so popular at Christmas. People get on to meet their country over the holidays."

This book includes stories, memoirs, articles, and poems that celebrate Christmas train journeys, describe what it was like to work on the railroad at Christmas time, and what it was like to play at Christmas time with the tiny trains set up beneath the tree, scale-model versions of the full-size marvels we never tired of watching. The text is accompanied by more than eighty illustrations: photos and paintings of trains on Christmas errands, pictures of stations and terminals at Christmas time, and copies of advertisements placed in national magazines by the railroads and the Pullman company that portrayed Christmas rail journeys alluringly. Covers and pages from the catalogs issued by the Lionel Corporation and American Flyer, the principal manufacturers of toy electric trains are here, as are brief profiles of the companies' founders: Joshua Lionel Cowen and A. C. Gilbert. In chapter four, *Home for Christmas*, the author describes a trip taken with his parents and brother from New York to the family home in northern Vermont, an overnight passage on the Montrealer that is recalled distinctly nearly sixty years later.

A Pennsylvania Railroad ad from the December 11, 1948, issue of *The Saturday Evening Post*. It's interesting to note the juxtaposition of the "modern" train and the horse-drawn sleigh that Grandma and Grandpa are using to carry their loved ones home.

If your pulse still quickens at the memory of such storied carriers as the Broadway Limited, the Super Chief, the California Zephyr, and the Twentieth Century Limited, there is much here for you to savor. If you cherish Christmas you will delight in these stories. The intent of this book is to remember good times, and rekindle a sense of wonder; the wonder of childhood Christmases, the trains that carried us to Christmas, and the trains that captured our imagination.

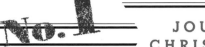

T he kinship between trains and Christmas dates back to Christmas Day, 1830, the time of the very first regularly scheduled passenger train trip in the United States. Undertaken by the South Carolina Canal and Railroad Company, the journey encompassed just six miles, from downtown Charleston, South Carolina, to the city limits, and then back again. Five open-air coaches were drawn by "The Best Friend of Charleston," a locomotive built at the West Point Foundry in New York and nicknamed by local businessmen already alert to the invention's commercial potential. The engine was about the size of a small pickup truck, and it rolled on four large wheels with wooden spokes. Its boiler and smokestack were configured vertically, the shape tapering at the top to create an

OPPOSITE Philadelphia's Broad Street Station in 1895, swarming with holiday-bound travelers. Author, bon vivant, and train devotee Lucius Beebe wrote that Broad Street was "one of the truly great railroad stations in the world, not because of either its architecture or volume of traffic, but because it personified the character of the carrier itself," in this case the mighty Pennsylvania Railroad.

impression of an oversized beer bottle.

A crowd of festively dressed citizens boarded the bunting-draped coaches and sat, no doubt a bit warily, as the "Best Friend" hissed and shuddered into motion. An account of the pioneering junket appeared two days later in the *Charleston Courier:*

> *The one hundred and forty-one persons flew on the wings of wind at the speed of fifteen to twenty-five miles per hour, annihilating time and space . . . leaving all the world behind . . . On the return we . . . darted forth like a live rocket, scattering sparks and flames on either side, passed over three salt creeks hop, step, and jump, and landed safe at the Lines before any of us had time to determine whether or not it was prudent to be scared.*

Many family gatherings later that day were flavored with excited talk about the puffing contraption and the breathless rate of speed at which it traveled. Passenger train travel had made its debut, and it could hardly have chosen a more felicitous day to do so.

Christmas day, 1830. Some citizens of Charleston, South Carolina, are about to embark on the first regularly scheduled passenger train trip in U.S. history. Note the horses at the far left of the picture, perhaps frightened by the smoking monster, or perhaps aware that a new age was upon them. Horatio Allen, the line's chief engineer, had argued for the use of the locomotive in place of horsepower. "There was no reason to expect any material improvement in the breed of horses," he said, "while in my judgment the man was not living who knew what breed of locomotives was to place at command."

By 1850, just two decades later, the six-mile route in South Carolina had spawned rail lines that extended more than 9,000 miles throughout several eastern states. New England was one of the first regions to be linked by rails. The author and naturalist Henry David Thoreau loved to watch the trains clattering through the Massachusetts woodlands near his home. During a Christmas blizzard he described the heroic passage of a Boston-bound flyer: "On this morning of the great snow, perchance which is still raging and chilling men's blood, I hear the muffled tone of their unique bell from out the fog bank of their chilled breath, which announces that the cars are coming, without long delay, notwithstanding the veto of a New England northeast snowstorm."

By the 1920s, railroads stretched to every corner of the nation, numbering nearly a quarter of a million miles, and passenger travel had entered "a golden age," with luxury carriers speeding between cities, their preeminence unchallenged, for the most part, by automobiles and airplanes. Shortly before Christmas in 1928, the Twentieth Century Limited, pride of the New York Central, traveled westbound from New York City to Chicago in seven separate sections. A few days after Christmas, the eastbound Century ran again in seven sections. It was reported that all sections, in both directions, arrived on or ahead of time.

Holiday travel was, by this time, sufficiently institutionalized to prompt some irreverent chronicling. Humorist Robert Benchley, writing in 1927, anticipated a yuletide sojourn with substantial misgivings:

> *Hurray, hurray! Off to the country for Christmas! Pack up all the warm clothes in the house for you will need them up there where the air is*

A magazine ad from 1896, placed by the Lake Shore and Michigan Southern Railway. A solitary traveler is greeted by his hosts along with the family pet. The train is receding into the distance, and horse-drawn sleighs and coaches are in evidence.

OVERLEAF, LEFT The New York Central was among the more prolific transport advertisers during the 1940s and 1950s. Artist Leslie Ragan portrayed the Twentieth Century Limited in many settings, but never more splendidly than in this nocturnal passage.

LESLIE
RAGAN

clean and cold. In order to get to East Russet you take the Vermont Central as far as Twitchell's Falls and change there for Torpid River Junction, where a spur line takes you right into Gormley. At Gormley you are met by a buckboard which takes you back to Torpid River Junction again. By this time a train or something has come in which will wait for the local from Beesus. While waiting for this you will have time to send your little boy to school, so that he can finish the third grade.

E. M. Frimbo, the self-proclaimed world's greatest railroad buff, was the alter ego of Rogers E. M. Whitaker, an editor at *The New Yorker*. Frimbo's delightful articles recounting his rail journeys around the world appeared in the magazine for years. He shared some of Benchley's yuletide disaffection by celebrating Christmas in what he called splendid isolation on a train bound for nowhere in particular. When someone at a holiday party asked his host where Mr. Frimbo was, he was told: "You seem to have forgotten that this is the time of year Frimbo goes into his annual retreat. Right now he's on a train somewhere, shut away in his bedroom, with the lights turned off."

American composer Alec Wilder was another holiday refugee. He loved trains and habitually carried a New York Central timetable in his jacket pocket, which abetted impulsive retreats. He was especially likely to disappear during the holidays, because of his dislike of all the sentiment that accompanied the season. When telephone service was introduced on the Central's Twentieth Century Limited, he delighted in calling some friends and neighbors in Rochester to wish them a merry Christmas, maintaining a safe distance between himself and the yuletide rites. One of these friends said that Wilder's idea at Christmas "was to be in the middle of nowhere, really in the middle of nowhere, say Manitoba in Canada on Christmas Day. . . . He loathed Christmas, the quintessential family holiday."

The South Shore Line, operating between Chicago and South Bend, Indiana, commissioned some stunning artwork for print and poster advertisements during the 1920s. Otto Brennemann, the artist, became a technical artist while serving in the German army during World War I. He emigrated to the United States after the war. When asked to comment on the future of American poster art, he said: "I wish that the American people might show more discrimination in the qualities of the arts and appreciate rather the original thought of an artistic creation than merely its superficial exterior."

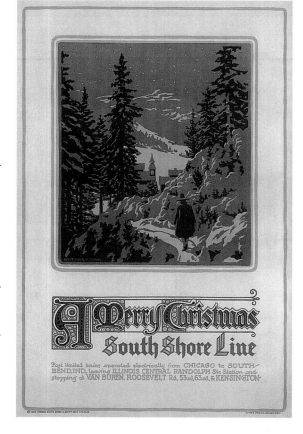

OPPOSITE On Christmas morning in 1956 a small group of youngsters and an excited pooch salute the passage of New York Central train No. 272, the Pittsburgh-Buffalo express. It stopped in such towns as Wampum, Pennsylvania, and Andover, Ohio, which hadn't seen a passenger train in a long time. The painting is by Howard Fogg.

PAGE 18 During the decade following World War II, many railroads promoted their passenger service in newspapers and magazines with vivid artwork and copy, none more so than the New York Central. The train in this picture bears the colors of the Twentieth Century Limited, but the drumhead identification is missing, lending a more generic flavor. Whatever the train, Santa seems proud to salute it.

Still another escapee, in this case from December's icy grip, was the novelist and short-story writer William Maxwell, who wrote the following rhapsody for *The New Yorker:*

My wife and I are planning to spend the first Christmas of our married life in Oregon with her mother and father. We have been living in a small, one-story house in northern Westchester County. It started to snow at dusk the evening before our departure and it has snowed all night. The view from the kitchen window is cribbed from John Greenleaf Whittier. The town snowplows have kept our road open and a taxi delivers us at Harmon station in plenty of time, but for the last hour no trains have come into or left the station. The ticket agent is noncommittal. We wait and wait, consult the station clock, count our luggage. Privately I entertain the possibility that we will spend this Christmas at home. At that moment, far down the tracks to the south, there is a light.

"The Twentieth Century Limited to Chicago arriving on Track Four!" the ticket agent announces over the public-address system, and in no time at all we are in our snug compartment looking out at the snow falling on the Hudson River. We are off. We have got away. Upstate New York, Pennsylvania, Ohio, and Indiana are like a long, uninterrupted, white thought. In Chicago the slush is ankle deep. Then we pick up the thought where we left off. It is winter all the way across the Great Plains and the Rocky Mountains, but in Portland there is no snow on the ground and the camellias are in bloom.

Bob Withers, a feature writer for the Huntington, West Virginia, *Herald-Dispatch* sought no escape from holiday festivities or the weather when he set out from his home in Huntington in mid-December of 1966, headed for the major rail junction at Cumberland, Maryland to see "B&O passenger trains swelled by Christmas traffic, mail and express cars packed with Christmas cards and gifts, coaches heavily laden with holiday travelers, and comfortable sleeping cars filled to capacity." Just before reaching Cumberland he decided, on a whim, to double back. He caught a train heading in the direction he'd just come from in order to see the mountains of western Maryland in the daytime. He also hoped for a snowfall to transform the rugged terrain into a Christmas card.

"...and to all a Good Night"

Any night's a good night for a "Winter's Nap" on the Water Level Route

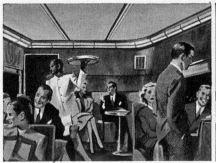

You go, weather or no!

Out there in the darkness, winter storm clouds may be scudding low above the tree tops. But aboard your New York Central train, you can depend on all the things that mean a good night. Good food in the diner. Good company and good cheer in the club lounge. And a good bed waiting for you.

Of beds and roadbeds

Drift off to sleep in the quiet privacy of your room . . . cradled by a deep mattress, rubber-cushioned couplers, stabilized car springs and roller bearings as you speed over a smooth, rock-ballasted roadbed through gentle, water-level valleys.

Good nights—good mornings!

Awake refreshed. Dress at leisure in your own completely equipped room. Then, an appetite-rousing New York Central breakfast . . . and you arrive with energy at peak, and not a business hour lost on your overnight vacation!

The Gift of Sleep is yours on the Great Steel Fleet

NEW DREAMLINERS in Production

Cars enough for 30 new all-room trains are on the way to spotlight the NEW in New York Central.

© 1946, New York Central Railroad Co.

NEW YORK CENTRAL

The Water Level Route—You Can Sleep

Thanks to a summer spent as an apprentice brakeman and flagman, Withers had made some friendly acquaintances with train workers along the B&O line, one of whom, an engineer named Lawrence Robey, invited Withers to ride along in the engine cab. At one stop along the westbound route Robey referred to Withers as a B&O official in order to explain his presence in the cab. The train continued, Withers living every young man's fantasy. Soon it began to snow, and snow very hard, impairing visibility and turning the tracks into sled runs. At one point, when the train was routed onto a siding to allow another train to pass, the snowfall was so heavy that Withers was asked to relay signals from the brakeman in the

A popular holiday song includes the lyrics "from Atlantic to Pacific, gee the traffic is terrific." This picture by Grif Teller verifies the sentiment. The setting is the Pennsylvania Railroad's route over the Susquehanna River at Harrisburg. The stone-arch, four-track span was built in 1902, and is the longest and widest bridge of its kind in the world. The train in the foreground is headed east, the passenger train on the left is curving toward Pittsburgh, and the third is turning north on its way to Buffalo.

The late Ted Rose titled this haunting study *The Shenandoah*, after one of the B&O's passenger carriers. The setting is Cumberland, Maryland, on a snowy afternoon in late December of 1950. The artist's notes explain that the diesel-powered consist is obscured by the assisting steam locomotive.

rear to the engineer. What a chance, he thought, to actually return a favor to a crew that had shown him so much of the Christmas spirit.

A day later Withers returned to his planned itinerary and made it to Cumberland. The station's roof, gables, and platform sheds were covered with a fresh mantle of snow. Christmas carols wafted through the waiting room's public address system, courtesy of the ticket agent's personal record collection. Withers spent the night watching the stately parade of some legendary carriers: the Cincinnati-bound National Limited, the eastbound Washington Express, the westbound Diplomat, and the eastbound Capitol Limited, the pride of the B&O, departing at 6:56 AM with four diesel units and eighteen coaches and sleeping cars filled with holiday travelers. Later that day, as his homebound train rumbled along the banks of the Ohio River, Withers shut his eyes and saw himself in the train's cab, searching the right-of-way ahead and tugging on the whistle cord.

Another solitary traveler, J. Thomas Staab, was a nineteen-year-old personnel clerk stationed at Malmstrom Air Force Base near Great Falls, Montana, in 1957. On Christmas Day, clutching a five-day pass, he caught the Great Northern Railway's Western Star, en route to Seattle, where he would transfer to a train that would take him to visit friends in Vancouver. The first leg of the trip proceeded along the south edge of Glacier National Park, whose snowy peaks were framed magnificently in the train's vista dome car. Staab's finances were meager. He ate a light breakfast and skipped lunch; and when the conductor asked why he'd missed the midday meal, Staab explained his situation. The conductor nodded, then said quietly, "I'm not supposed to tell you, but the Great Northern Railway always gives you Christmas dinner free. Just go back to the diner and order whatever you want." Staab ordered the biggest steak on the menu, followed by dessert and coffee. He then sat back and hoped for the best. The waiter approached bearing a check and wearing a smile, and to Staab's relief told him that the meal was a Christmas present from the Great Northern. Almost forty years later, Staab and his wife, aboard Amtrak's Empire

THE
GEORGE
WASHINGTON
THE SPORTSMAN
THE F. F. V.

George Washington's Railroad
CHESAPEAKE and OHIO Lines
Original Predecessor Company Founded by George Washington in 1785

The Ticket Agent of Any Railroad Can Route You on the Finest Fleet of Genuinely Air-Conditioned Trains in the World. Insist upon it!

Builder, traveled from Portland, Oregon, to Chicago, crossing some of the same territory Staab had covered in 1957. There were no free meals, but for Staab there was an indelible Christmas memory.

Dining cars, especially those assigned to pre-Amtrak carriers, occupy a precious place in our memories of train travel. Few railroads realized a profit on dining-car operations, but most maintained them with high levels of luxury and pride. Gary Dolzall was fourteen years old on Christmas Eve in 1967 when he and his family boarded the Super Chief, the flagship of the Atchison, Topeka, and Santa Fe Railroad, at their home station in Streator, Illinois, bound for a family reunion in California. Dolzall remembers that he slept very little that night, thanks to the excitement engendered by the Super Chief's passage, and the anticipation of Christmas. Christmas morning found the family seated at a table in the dining car. There was a wreath on the bulkhead, snow-white napery, Mimbreno china, and a fresh yellow rose on every table. Aromas of hot coffee, bacon, and pancakes filled the car, and the Fred

Holiday merriment in the club car. A hint of class distinction appears in the first paragraph of the ad copy where we read that "many" of the lounge cars are available to coach passengers "too." The ad appeared on the back cover of the December 1948 issue of *Trains* magazine.

OPPOSITE Artist Howard Fogg loved the Christmas season, and many of his paintings evoke the holidays. There is just a hint of snow in this scene set in the western plains, but an ad for a Christmas dance is nailed to a light pole, and two wreaths are in evidence, one in the observation-car window above the drumhead. A small boy is waving out of the window to a station worker who is returning the friendly greeting.

OPPOSITE It doesn't always snow on Christmas, but this painting by Ted Rose conveys the chill of a late-1940s December evening. Seen here are two sections of the Santa Fe's Super Chief, the extra-fare, all-Pullman train that covered the distance between Chicago and Los Angeles in 39½ hours during its glory years. This perspective is from Chicago's Roosevelt Road.

Years before the Dolzall family headed west on the Super Chief for their family reunion in 1967, the Santa Fe was placing ads in major magazines in hopes of enticing travelers. This one ran in the *National Geographic* in November 1949.

Give your family the **Sun** for Christmas

Go **Santa Fe to Phoenix, Wickenburg, Palm Springs and Southern California**

You've promised yourself to take the family on a winter vacation sometime. This is the year! Why not make it your Christmas present to them? The resorts and ranches in sunny Arizona and Southern California are beckoning, and Santa Fe's famous fleet of fine trains to these "sun spots" offers schedules and accommodations to suit you to a "T."

Santa Fe

Santa Fe System Lines, Room 1753, Dept. NG-8
80 East Jackson Boulevard, Chicago 4, Illinois
Please send me your free directory of Winter Resorts and Ranches in the Southwest.

NAME_____
ADDRESS_____
CITY AND STATE_____
*If student, give name of school*_____

Expires May 31, 1950

Harvey waiters bustled about like skaters, taking orders and balancing trays laden with glorious breakfast fare. Dolzall thought that the bacon served on the Super Chief was unsurpassed. Later that day, watching the sun set from his roomette window, Dolzall was treated to the sight of the eastbound Super Chief, passing just a few feet away. "I watched and I knew there could be no finer end to that magic day," he wrote.

Greg McDonnell, a firefighter from Kitchener, Ontario, reached his fifteenth birthday on Christmas Day in 1969. In an effort to make certain that both events received their due, his family typically celebrated his birthday in the morning, and Christmas in the evening. His birthday package contained a 35-millimeter camera, something he had hinted for tirelessly, but his Christmas present, sealed in a small gift envelope, was, for him, the ultimate prize. It was a round-trip railroad ticket from his home to Montreal, a city several hundred miles and an overnight trek away. There he would spend five days with a friend. Unlike Gary Dolzall, who traveled with his family, McDonnell was permitted to travel alone, quite a heady prospect for a young teenager. "The Canadian National's Kitchener station was crowded with holiday travelers that Christmas night, but it made no difference to me," McDonnell wrote years later, savoring every detail. "Regardless of the weather I always preferred to wait outside, pacing the platform, listening to the offbeat idle of the local yard engines and intently watching for a headlight to poke over the horizon."

Finally, and right on time, the Grand Trunk Western's Maple Leaf drew into the station, twelve hours out from Dearborn Station in Chicago. McDonnell clambered aboard, and, less than two hours later, arrived in Toronto, where he transferred to a Canadian

National train called the Cavalier. It was nearly midnight when the Cavalier departed Toronto, but sleep was the last thing on McDonnell's mind. "Economics dictated coach accommodations," he wrote, "but in truth, sleeping car space would have been wasted on a fifteen-year-old, who, with no intention of sleeping, spent the entire night wide awake, peering out the windows and fairly bursting with excitement."

A gray December dawn welcomed McDonnell to Montreal. He and his friend, wasting no time, boarded a local train for the town of Delson, where they visited the Canadian Railway Museum. The tour was cut short due to a heavy snowfall that forced them to return to Montreal at midday. By the following morning the city was buried in nearly two feet of snow, and a day later it was still snowing. Heedless of forecasts predicting the worst winter storm in the city's recent history, McDonnell and his friend plunged through the snow to the Montreal West station, where they watched crews struggling to keep trains moving through piles of drifting, blowing snow. One passenger train, the Atlantic Limited, inching slowly through coupler-deep drifts, its engine wheels spinning on the icy rails, eased to a stop at the platform, where it struck a pose for McDonnell's Christmas camera.

A day later the storm abated, and two days later it was time for McDonnell to return home. He and his friend had filled their daylight hours with as much train viewing, station visiting, and museum touring as the storm, and their pluck, permitted. The westbound Maple Leaf delivered McDonnell home on New Year's Eve. He stood on the platform for a lingering moment, watching his train recede into the winter twilight. He wrote, "I walked away from the station with a folder full of used tickets, a bag of exposed film, and a lifetime supply of happy memories."

No doubt McDonnell's family greeted him in a station decked with Christmas lights, garlands, wreaths, and other trimmings. North American railroad stations, from tiny rural depots to the most majestic urban palaces, were radiant at Christmas time. During the 1930s and 1940s, Grand Central Station in New York City was decorated with several towering Christmas trees, each one strung with five hundred lights, and a wreath, twenty-five feet in diameter, that hung above the ramp that led to the main waiting room. The wreath weighed a bit more than a ton, reportedly consumed a freight-car-load of evergreens and holly, its bright red ribbon was three feet wide, and, before being tied, a hundred yards long.

On a more modest scale, the B&O Railroad in its Wheeling, West Virginia, station, marked the season by giving out a sprig of holly with each ticket sold, and encouraging patrons to join with local choirs as they offered Christmas songs and carols.

OPPOSITE This snowy scene makes it possible for us to imagine the stubby train performing all manner of holiday chores. The scene is Bromptonville, Quebec, and the train is a Canadian National morning local from Sherbrooke to Montreal, running along the banks of the St. Francis River. The temperature was twenty-four degrees below zero and, according to Jim Shaughnessy, the photographer, "the steam hung in a great column long after the train had passed."

★ Dec. 11, 1954
THE NEW YORKER
Price 20 cents

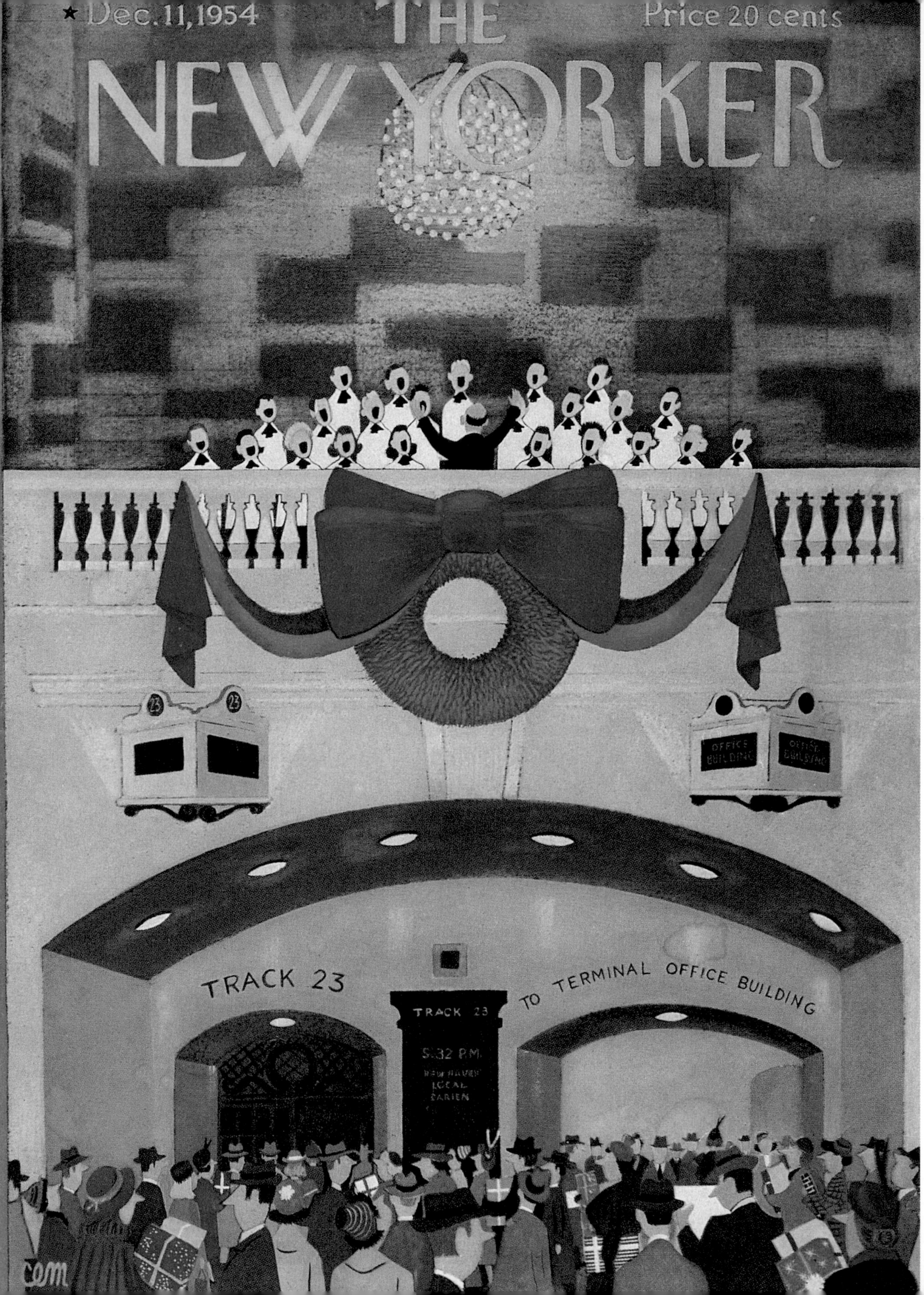

Holiday music was also heard in New York's Grand Central Station. City school and church choirs performed every evening throughout December during the 1930s and 1940s. The cheerful recitals were especially appreciated during the Depression and the dispiriting days of World War II. An editorial in the *New York Times* dated December 24, 1944, expressed the sentiments of millions: "Of all the customs that at this season lend happy refutation to the legend of New York's cold hardness none is pleasanter or more striking than the Christmas music that floats nightly over the hurrying concourse of Grand Central Station. The deep-throated notes of the organ and the clear tones of the young carolers come like a breath of hope and peace in a dismal world torn by war. Here pass to and fro the hasty steps of service men and women from all parts of the country; older men and women still doing their peacetime jobs and breathing a prayer for those dear to them who are absent and in danger; visitors from foreign lands. All are made kin for a fleeting instant by music as universal in its appeal as the message it brings. Hearts are made a little lighter and souls more peaceful because of it."

Impromptu sing-alongs also occurred in stations, and on trains as well. A week before Christmas in 1952, aboard a Rock Island commuter train leaving Chicago's LaSalle Street Station, a dapper gentleman in a topcoat and gray fedora took a concertina out of a case and launched into some joyful caroling. He was soon joined by everyone in the car. And for almost a decade during the 1940s, John P. Whalen, the vice president of the Society for the Preservation and Encouragement of Barbershop Quartets, joined three fellow choristers in Boston's North Station every day at 5:00 PM during the week before Christmas, and harmonized heartily, much to the

Christmas Window on the Water Level Route

Watch New York Central trains roll past this time of year. You'll see Christmas windows by the hundred ... bright with the most precious of all gifts. People!

Couples taking their children to see Grandmother (on money-saving Family Fares). Older folk, off to spend Christmas with married sons or daughters—enjoying every minute of New York Central comfort.

Youngsters from school or college getting a first taste of holiday fare in the dining car. Fathers, away on business, taking it easy in the club car ... sure that New York Central will get them home "weather or no."

These are the year's favorite jobs for New York Central men and women. So whether you ride with us or meet the train ... here's wishing you a MERRY CHRISTMAS!

Give Tickets—The Gift that Brings Them Home!
Ask any Central ticket agent how easy it is to send rail and Pullman tickets as your gift to someone you want with you at holiday time.

New York Central
The Water Level Route—You Can Sleep

This holiday scene highlights two of the New York Central's points of pride—family travel and the Water Level Route. Unlike its competitors who navigated mountainous terrain, the Central offered travel from New York to Chicago that ran through the Hudson and Mohawk River valleys, along the edge of Lake Erie, and around the southern tip of Lake Michigan.

OPPOSITE New York's Grand Central Station offered Christmas music for many years, provided by church and school choirs who sometimes performed concerts above the station's huge ribboned wreath.

Like the painting of the Super Chiefs by Ted Rose, this study by Grif Teller portrays the late-1940s transition from steam to diesel power. The trains, crowded with Christmas travelers, are running beside the Juniata River about twenty miles west of Harrisburg, Pennsylvania.

delight of weary shoppers and commuters.

Santa Claus also enlivened the scene in and around railroad stations during the holidays, and in the spirit of things he usually arrived by train. In Milwaukee, Wisconsin, from 1928 through 1955, Santa rode in a train over the city's streetcar tracks every first Saturday in December, heralding the start of the holiday season on behalf of the Schuster's department-store chain. The train consisted of a work engine decorated with an electric Christmas tree on its front, three flatcars stacked with holiday displays and playthings from Schuster's toy department, and Santa himself sitting on his sleigh and waving to all. Santa's helpers included Billie the Brownie, Willy Wagtail, and Metik the Eskimo, three characters from a popular children's radio show sponsored by Schuster's. Policemen astride snarling motorcycles escorted the train and added to the excitement.

In 1972 the tradition was revived in the town of East Troy, thirty-five miles southwest of Milwaukee. An engine and a pair of flatcars were decorated to look like Christmas floats, and Santa, with his sleigh and some plywood reindeer, rode on one of the cars, surrounded by elves wearing red caps, white tunics, and baggy green trousers. A pair of loudspeakers sounded "Jingle Bells" and "The Parade of the Wooden Soldiers,"

the same soundtrack used for the old Schuster's train. The procession paralleled County Trunk Highway ES for several miles, allowing some onlookers to greet its passage from their front porches, and ended at the railway's substation-museum-gift shop two blocks north of the village square.

Santa had a much longer ride over the Clinchfield Railroad line during the years following World War II. He traveled ninety-four miles between Elkhorn City, Kentucky, and Kingsport, Tennessee, representing members of the Kingsport Merchant's Bureau, who wanted to thank the people along the line for doing business in their city. The train stopped frequently en route and dispensed gifts, candy, and even firewood to hard-pressed miners and their families. For thirty-eight years, until 1984, John Dudney faithfully played the role of Santa, assisted for most of those years by E. B. "Jitney" Blankenbecler. One of Jitney's most important jobs was to try to make sure that some recipients did not partake of the goodies more than once. A few enterprising citizens would hop into their cars after gathering up their gifts and drive to the next stop, arriving ahead of the slow-moving train. On some narrow roads the practice became so dangerous for drivers and pedestrians alike that the police set up roadblocks to check licenses and perform vehicle inspections. In its peak years the Kingsport Santa Claus train visited nearly 25,000 people along its route, delivering six tons of gifts donated by the Kingsport merchants and well-wishers from around the country. As longtime helper Raymond Galyon said in 1989, "You'd think I'd be used to it by now, but every trip is like the first. I cry on every one of them."

This photo of the Clinchfield's Santa Claus train was taken near Rikemo, Virginia, in 1976. At that time the train had been a regional fixture for thirty years.

OPPOSITE A father and son have just chopped down their Christmas tree and are greeting the swift passage of a Norfolk & Western train in this photograph by O. Winston Link. Look closely and you'll see two more youngsters watching the train from the bank across the road.

While passengers sat, reclined, slept, and sometimes stood inside the coaches and Pullman cars spiriting them away to holiday destinations, thousands of railroad people dedicated themselves to on-time arrivals, as well as the swift delivery of tons of mail, packages, and freight. At Christmas, while home and family beckoned, railroad men and women coped with peak demands, almost invariably with efficiency and good cheer.

Setting the Christmas work mood, David P. Morgan, the longtime editor of *Trains*, wrote the following in the January 1965 issue of the magazine: "I recall a Christmas Eve years ago in Louisville, Kentucky, when an L&N J-1 2-8-2 came padding up through our Crescent Hill residential section over the quilt of a carpet of freshly-fallen snow, her soft exhaust trying not to disturb those who were decorating trees

OPPOSITE The title of this painting from the January 1951 issue of *Railroad* magazine is *Unscheduled Stop*. Artist Herb Mott has halted the little train to let one of the crew chop down a Christmas tree, which another crew member is beginning to decorate.

and filling stockings. The railroad couldn't relax, but it was tiptoeing about those who could on Yuletide."

The softly treading transport may well have been the L&N's train No. 1, the Azalean, southbound from Cincinnati, en route to New Orleans. It would have rumbled through Morgan's neighborhood around 9:30 PM, coinciding with Christmas Eve chores and cheer. During the early 1940s, the period recalled by Morgan, the Azalean carried coaches and sleeping cars from Cincinnati through to New Orleans, picked up another sleeper in Birmingham that originated in New York, a lounge car in Nashville that connected from Chicago, and a dining car "for all meals," as noted in the L&N timetable.

How the small and crowded kitchens on trains carrying hundreds of hungry passengers managed consistently to turn out excellent meals was always a mystery. Pictured here is a chef aboard a New York Central train starting to carve a Christmas turkey.

OPPOSITE Stoops Ferry, Pennsylvania, is the setting for this painting by Howard Fogg, titled *Christmas Mail, 1907.* Sixty years later, the U.S. Postal Service notified the nation's railroads that it was terminating all railway post-office contracts. It was a knockout punch to the already staggering passenger service in the United States.

The Christmas workday in the Azalean dining car began at 4:30 AM, when the third cook started the kitchen fire, using small logs of compressed sawdust. The rest of the crew reported thirty minutes later, emerging from their quarters in the dormitory car coupled next to the dining car. The regular menu would be available, but tucked into the oven were several turkeys, to be roasted through the morning and served for lunch and dinner. The L&N routinely served hundreds of turkey dinners on Christmas day, but was no match for the mighty Pennsylvania Railroad, which served 3,500 holiday feasts in 1951.

Even so, there were occasional lulls in the holiday schedule, which enabled Pullman and dining-car attendants to do some celebrating of their own. Virgil Smock, a Pullman buffet and lounge-car attendant from 1936

Christmas trees on the children's menu indicate a holiday meal aboard a Southern Pacific dining car in 1927.

OPPOSITE Various passenger-train jobs are depicted in this ad that appeared in the December 1950 issue of *National Geographic*. An HO train set is added to make the scene completely irresistible.

through 1960, recalled a few Christmases with light duties: "Christmas Eve or Christmas night, if a certain car didn't have nobody, and according to who the conductor was, we'd have a good time. We'd be sitting there, we'd be working my car, drinking egg nog and everything else you know."

All of the passenger carriers operating during the years following World War II took great pride in the care and feeding of their customers, especially at Christmas. The Union Pacific's "City" trains—City of Portland, City of Denver, City of San Francisco, and City of Los Angeles—included full dining and lounge cars on their runs; and from mid-December through early January they often carried as many as fifteen Pullman cars, with a dome lounge, dome diner, plus a "helper" diner and lounge to satisfy overflow thirst and hunger.

"Welcome aboard" circulars and flyers were placed in every sleeping-car accommodation. Matchbooks with a Christmas scene on one side, and a full-color drawing of a UP streamliner plowing through a snowfall, imprinted with "Merry Christmas from the Union Pacific," were set next to ashtrays in the lounge car. Lounge and dining cars were festooned with ornaments, wreaths, and pine boughs, and holiday music was heard through the train's public-address system.

Dining-car chefs were encouraged to express their creativity at Christmas time, and the smoked turkey and mincemeat and pumpkin pies served in

UP dining cars were especially memorable. In the club cars and lounges, bartenders offered holiday potables, including Christmas old-fashioneds that fueled merriment well into the night.

John Gohmann, working as a brakeman for the UP to defray college costs, was called out on Christmas Eve in 1966 to work the City of Los Angeles, eastbound out of Omaha. He deadheaded from his home in Marion, Iowa, to Omaha on the City of Denver, and on the way was treated to a Christmas Eve feast of smoked turkey with raspberry dressing, creamy mashed potatoes, squash, crisp green beans, and pumpkin pie. The train reached Omaha shortly before 11:00 PM, and after a nap Gohmann donned his uniform and greeted the passengers boarding in Omaha's stately Union Station for their 3:40 AM departure.

The City of Los Angeles, powered by five E9 diesel engines, and carrying twenty-one cars, departed Omaha on the minute. During his first inspection tour of the train, Gohmann discovered a little boy and his dad in the dome car. The youngster said that they were watching for Santa's sleigh. The dome was officially closed between midnight and 6:00 AM, but Gohmann didn't have the heart to disrupt a Santa watch. Instead, he told the child that he'd just spoken with the engineer, who mentioned that Santa had been spotted flying over Nebraska a few hours earlier, and might have worked his way further east by now. He encouraged the boy to keep watching.

At 6:30 the first call to breakfast sounded. The dining-car steward greeted the ladies with a long-stemmed rose, a traditional UP Christmas morning welcome. Complimentary glasses of champagne would be offered at lunchtime. Gohmann and his fellow crew members had time for breakfast, a serving of the Union Pacific's celebrated French toast, before reaching their crew-change stop in Marion. Gohmann's parents were at the station; they told him how much they'd missed him the night before, the first time he had not been home on Christmas Eve. "I missed you both too," he said, "but you missed something very special that I'll never forget, and that was Christmas morning on the City of Los Angeles."

OPPOSITE Santa's bounty is overflowing in this cheerful ad placed by the Missouri Pacific Railroad. The MOPAC's Texas Eagle carried a dome car fancifully called "Planetarium" between San Antonio and St. Louis. On this Christmas Eve the coach is filled with holiday pilgrims of all ages.

Another marquee train, the California Zephyr, operating between Chicago and San Francisco, provided the most spectacular settings for Christmas pilgrimages anywhere in the country. The trip included glimpses of skiers on Colorado slopes, a view of the Wasatch mountain range in Utah, and a spellbinding, 116-mile ride through the Sierra Nevada's Feather River Canyon. Zephyr crews marked the holidays by placing live Colorado spruce trees in the observation cars, holly on the dining-car tables, and wreaths in the club cars. On many trips a crew member donned a Santa Claus suit and roamed the length of the train, dispensing yuletide greetings.

Amtrak retained the name, if not the Zephyr's grandeur, when it took over passenger service in 1971. Following is an account of a holiday working trip in 1988, written by William B. Francik, Jr., a former Amtrak car attendant, and a trustee of the Chicago chapter of the National Railway Historical Society.

Sixty years before Francik's run, during the late 1920s when passenger-train travel enjoyed peak patronage, stations and terminals in America's major cities were alive with practically round-the-clock comings and goings, and were especially busy at Christmas. At Chicago's Union Station the Chicago, Burlington & Quincy Railroad designated 5:15 PM as "Burlington Hour," and on Christmas Eve in 1927 its timetable proclaimed the hour's import: "5:15 PM! The busiest moment of the fullest hour in the pulsating life of the splendid Chicago Union Station presents the striking spectacle of four great Burlington trains drawn up on contiguous tracks-steamup-personnel on the qui-vive! It is doubtful that such a galaxy of crack trains is gathered together in one moment on any other railroad anywhere else in America. Every one of the four is a distinguished, deluxe train—a thoroughbred stripped for action."

A card sent in 1939—hence the reference to track 39 in the verse—by the Chicago and North Western Railway Company to some of its customers. The company mascot is illustrated, and the signer, Carl R. Gray, Jr., was probably a high-ranking CNW official.

Working Amtrak's California Zephyr is never really easy, no matter the season, no matter your craft. Sleeping-car and coach attendants, waiters, cooks, dining-car stewards, and barmen share the same lot during the seemingly eternal pull from Chicago to Oakland and back. You put in twenty-hour days under cramped conditions with a continuously fluid mix of passengers, people who shuffle countless wild cards into that deck you call your job. Yet that first night out goes quickly, with rapid-fire stops at Naperville, Princeton, and Galesburg, Illinois. Each stop can be tumultuous, even riotous, as a crush of humanity attempts to step off the cars while others ford the crowd to get aboard.

"Step back, folks! Give 'em room to get off," you command in your most authoritarian voice. "No visitors on the train, please. All passengers up the stairs and to the right," you shout above the din.

Each station takes you farther and farther from home and the life led by "normal people," nonrailroaders who enjoy nine-to-five days, five-day work weeks, weekends free, and holidays at home with family and friends.

Then it's Iowa. We rumble across the Mississippi River and stop at Burlington. Beyond are Mount Pleasant, Ottumwa, Osceola, and Creston, rushing at you as train 5 (Burlington Northern calls her "1005") slices through a frigid Hawkeye State shrouded in winter's early, deep, dark cloak of night. The outline of the train looks like a Lionel set strung around a huge Christmas tree, complete with tiny towns and silhouettes of people in the coach windows.

New faces, ripe with December's holiday anticipation, board at every depot. Wind-burned cheeks, numb fingers, and sniffling noses are telltale signs of Midwestern win-

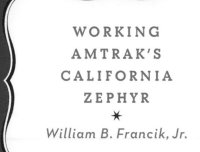

WORKING AMTRAK'S CALIFORNIA ZEPHYR

*

William B. Francik, Jr.

ter winds, bitter and blustery. Red noses are made even more runny once inside the warm, dry coaches. Suitcases, backpacks, trunks, boxes, and shopping bags stuffed with gifts, snacks, and six-packs come aboard. Fresh faces displace those that became vaguely familiar in a short while: tit-for-tat, twenty off, twenty-two on, a scramble for seats, hopefully in pairs so that couples and families can share the ride. "Fat chance tonight," you think. After prodding, a high-school kid, complete with the seemingly mandatory high-top Reeboks and faded denims, reluctantly relinquishes a coveted double. "Sorry, this is the holiday season. We need every seat. Please move your things so this nice (two hundred-pound, sixty-year-old) lady can have a seat," you explain diplomatically. The teen sulks and moves his coat and Walkman as he stares at you with eyes that are either mournful or murderous—it's a thin line. His face might plaintively implore you to sit an attractive young blonde next to him, but you're thinking, "Sorry, life is tough sometimes."

You really wish you could do better for both passengers, but you've got a family aboard to worry about. A cherubic-faced father asks for seats together for his wife and kids. You play musical chairs and somehow accomplish the impossible, seating the two children across the aisle from their parents. When you return with fresh pillows for the youngsters, Mom and Dad are holding hands. Dad offers you a couple of bucks. But they look like they're struggling to make ends meet, so you refuse the offer. "That's O.K. Drop it in the collection plate on Christmas" seems like the right thing to say . . . and you do.

Your home away from home is a thirteen-car stainless-steel string of mostly double-deck Superliner cars led by the 6,000 horses of two EMD F40PH diesels. The crew will work, eat, sleep, and smile as if on cue aboard this land-borne cruise ship, complete with captain—the conductor. Actually, it resembles a submarine more than some luxury liner, given the tight confines. However, submariners don't have to deal with the public. The on-board crew, under the direction of the Service Chief, works straight through from Chicago to Oakland, a scheduled fifty-one-hour trip, before returning to the Windy City, after which they get as few as two days off before starting all over again. Engine and train crews, now also all Amtrak employees, change out seven times on the 2,422-mile run.

If you're working coach (which I favor), you will sack five hundred pillows round trip, meaning you'll cycle five hundred different guests aboard your car during your turn. You will tote thousands of pounds of luggage and try to keep the car reasonably clean, but you realize early on that you are not working for Swiss Federal Railways serving "considerate passengers." Americans are not, shall we say, tidy.

Omaha comes awfully late but the throngs are out in force. Someone says a recent storm has closed the airport. No. 5 may be running an hour late, but our craft is the only way west out of town tonight. We're jammed to the rafters as six hundred souls entrust their holiday travels to the National Railroad Passenger Corporation. Soon we're off and running again.

One hour of tortuous wrestling with fatigue finally is relieved as the train arrives in Lincoln. Once we're out of here you can get some sleep. The Cornhusker State capital is home for the only unicameral state legislature, a distinction matched in uniqueness by the singular pleasure of standing trainside to detrain and entrain passengers at 1:00 AM as the thermometer quivers at three degrees Fahrenheit. "Joy to the World." The air bites at all exposed flesh. God, but it's cold! Your mind pleads,

"Let's get going so I can close up this door and crash."

With your passengers finally in their seats for the night and the conductor informed about where you'll be sleeping (Room B in the dormitory car up front), you retire for some badly needed rest. The second day out is a L-O-N-G one, twenty hours minimum, so you'll need every minute of sleep you can get. If your car boards any passengers at the likes of Hastings, Holdrege, or McCook, the attendant in the next car, or another crew member, probably will cover for you . . . as you will do for others, in turn. Exhausted, you finally lie down. You dream of home.

All too quickly Denver is at your doorstep, the skyline of the city accented by the Rocky Mountains looming to the west. It is an awesome sight. How could anyone tire of this view, once enjoyed from the Vista Domes of the pre-Amtrak California and Denver Zephyrs.

Almost half the car turns over at Denver, so you'll be getting at least thirty-five new passengers. Denver Union Terminal ("DUT" to old timers) is a chaotic bazaar of people, high-wheeled baggage carts dutifully following tractors, through-passengers stretching their legs on the platform, and mechanical crews poking around the cars trying to make the inevitable repairs, usually with that railroad maid-of-all-work tool, the hammer. "Can you guys restore the toilets in the next coach up from mine?" you inquire of a foreman. "We'll try," comes the reply, "but don't count on it." You never do. Meanwhile, car men scurry around with stiff water hoses, slaking the thirsts of nearly empty water tanks on each car. Six hundred guests use lots of water.

Curiously, the Zephyr's holiday-swollen consist doesn't warrant a third road engine west out of Denver this morning. Our two F40PH's will be on their own on the Denver & Rio Grande Western as they assault the

A view of the California Zephyr painted by Howard Fogg. For years the train carried five dome-observation cars, in order to afford every passenger a view of the train's magnificent route. The stairway to the dome seats in the first-class lounge-observation car, which is prominent in this picture, was illuminated by tiny spotlights and luminous Lucite handrails that cast a golden glow.

long 2 percent ruling grade around the Big Ten Loops, through the foothills of the Rockies, then along the challenging climb to the Continental Divide. The F40s will make it, but there won't be much power to spare.

After a doting oil truck tops off each locomotive's 1800-gallon fuel tank—a prudent precaution prior to a 570-mile run to the next refueling stop in Salt Lake City—the mechanical crews make some important last checks and clean the headlights and windshields before pulling down the blue flags that protect the train while men are at work on and under it. With the last of the passengers aboard, the Zephyr is ready to resume its California journey. At 10:25 AM (MST), after the conductor bellows a ritualistic "Boooard," the hogger in the lead F40 responds with two sharp, short hoots, and the double-deck train begins to crawl out of town. The wheels step through numerous switches out of DUT, tiptoeing before they can run free over cold steel ribbons going west.

We are one hour, thirty minutes tardy out of DUT, yet no one seems to care. We are about to enjoy the unsurpassed splendor of the Rio Grande's main line across Colorado and Utah. "Grandeur on the Grande." It's simply picture-perfect. Brilliant! A holiday greeting-card scene is painted with crystalline, powdered snow, an azure sky, and starched, puffy clouds set in piercing, antiseptic sunlight.

Soon, 5 breaks free of the jumbled sprawl of Denver, and our spirited train sprints out of the Platte River Valley before it's brought to a noticeable crawl again. Suddenly gravity's grip is apparent as it slows the Zephyr's first steps into the foothills. But our power is up to the task and the rope of cars snakes around the Little Ten and then Big Ten curves. Passengers once oblivious to the train's progress suddenly are riveted to the windows, fingers pointing and camera shutters firing away.

Plainview siding allows us to see Denver 1,500 feet below to the east. And then No. 5 begins to thread through Tunnel 1, the first of twenty-nine bores on the Grande's "Tunnel District."

We proceed along one of railroading's most fascinating alignments. Sometimes our long train rolls through two tunnels simultaneously as we steadily climb, feeling our way along the slender bench blasted out of the sheer granite slabs that mark the eastern face of the Rocky Mountains. The Great Plains are behind us and far below as our train penetrates South Boulder Canyon. At Rollinsville we meet a waiting 110-car coal train, a lumbering behemoth powered by four big black Rio Grande units up front and two midtrain. The coal drag is a smudged, all-business, money-making affair bound for some Texas electric utility. The freight's engine crew waves as we sneak past. Two preschoolers wave back enthusiastically.

The dining-car crew is closing down after serving breakfast to nearly three hundred passengers. The diner opened at 6:00 AM, stayed open for business right through the hour-long Denver stop despite being without head-end power during some of the layover, and finally closed at 11:00. Now the crew is rushing to set up for what will surely be a huge lunch crowd. The holidays demand stamina, patience, and teamwork. Four cooks, four waiters, and the steward did their best to keep up with the breakfast crowd as the most popular meal of the day put them to the test. But this crew was up to it—they can move!

Up ahead is a 6.2-mile long Moffat Tunnel, the fourth-longest railroad bore in the Western Hemisphere. Once inside, the CZ will attain its highest altitude at 9,239 feet directly under Rollins Pass. Just short of the needle's eye that marks the base of the Continental Divide, though, 5 comes to a halt. The giant exhaust fans at Moffat's eastern portal are purging the tunnel of diesel fumes from another westbound train that has just cleared the big hole's western end. The high-pitched whine of the fans disturbs the peace surrounding an otherwise placid, if frozen, meadow.

The Zephyr waits patiently, obediently, at Milepost 50.1. The clear sky is obscured by fine snow whipped around by razor-sharp gusts off the towering granite divide. The crew goes about its tasks while the passengers settle down again, preoccupied with thoughts of holidays past or plans for the season at hand. Most are unaware of the drama of running a thirteen-car hotel over tough mountain terrain, across vast deserts, through bad weather. The passengers are on their way to family and friends, or to be with someone special for the holidays. The crew? They will work through yet another Hanukkah, Christmas, or New Year's just as if they were any other days. They hope to grab some time at home once they return on "day six." In the meantime, there is work to do, a living to earn.

After several minutes, 5 gets a green from the lineside signal. The Moffat Tunnel is clear. Whistling off, the engineer opens the throttle and the Zephyr accelerates. Heat waves and dark exhaust rise from each unit, swallowed up by the frigid alpine air. The train heads into the dark bore and wends its way through the holidays.

The drama of the season and its players—passengers, crew, and, yes, the railroad—blend into an intoxicating elixir that goes down easily. It tugs at the heart and etches the soul.

I am blessed. I have tasted it. I have savored its rich flavor. And I probably always will.

The four great trains were the Denver Limited, the Missouri Limited bound for Kansas City, the Nebraska Limited headed for Omaha and Lincoln, and the Black Hawk, on the St. Paul and Minneapolis route.

Two decades later this level of activity was exceeded substantially in the Los Angeles Union Passenger Terminal. Beginning at 12:30 AM on the day before Christmas, thirty-one trains departed between that hour and 11:30 PM; and between 6:00 AM and 10:55 PM thirty-one trains arrived. These included such storied streamliners as the Santa Fe's Chief, Super Chief, and El Capitán; the Southern Pacific's San Joaquin Daylight and Golden State; and the City of Los Angeles, wearing Union Pacific colors.

For all the railroad people routinely encountered by travelers, there were a great many more less frequently seen—the engineers, firemen, brakemen, and other passenger and freight-train crew members whose anonymous tasks served the trains as vitally as any uniformed attendant's, perhaps more so. The engineer was, of course, the captain, the master, the lordly figure piloting the train. He was the idol of millions of youngsters who imagined themselves at the controls, tugging on the whistle cord, and returning the waves of young and old alike.

On Christmas Eve of 1939, F. E. Wells, an engineer on the SOO Line, was unexpectedly called out to drive an engine on a freight train running from his home in Chippewa Falls, Wisconsin, to Minneapolis. Wells was resting in his favorite chair when he got the phone call, and argued to no avail with the yard foreman. He thought he had logged enough extra hours before Christmas to ensure a quiet holiday at home. He did manage to talk the foreman into assigning him the fastest engine in the roundhouse, an accomplishment that served him well later that evening.

Wells reported to the yard, carrying two thick turkey sandwiches, climbed aboard his locomotive, and made the run to Minneapolis in less than two hours, a breathless schedule for a long, fully loaded freight. His determination to return home before Christmas morning was contagious. His crew assumed the duties of adding coal and water to the steam engine, chores that would ordinarily be handled by yard workers, except late on Christmas Eve. They turned the engine on the turntable by attaching a hose to the engine's air supply, and pointed it for the return run to Chippewa Falls.

But the next hurdle, finding someone to cut orders for the engine's return late on Christmas Eve, proved much more difficult to clear. Wells used the yard phone and called the division manager working that night, and was thrilled to hear the voice of a friend. His friend was sympathetic to Wells's wish to return home, but refused to release the engine, for fear that Wells, throttle-high, would drive it into a cornfield. Wells hung up the phone, his hopes dashed. He began

This notice ran in the December 1944 issue of *Fortune* magazine. A year earlier, a similar reminder appeared in *Fortune*, but with a more lenient deadline of December tenth.

Have you sent your Christmas packages?

MAKE December 1st YOUR SHIPPING DATE!

The Association of American Railroads, the industry's governing body, aware that package-delivery anxieties ran especially high at Christmas time, placed this reassuring message "Our railroads help make Christmas merry," in the December 1, 1946, issue of the *Saturday Evening Post*.

a slow walk back to the roundhouse, and on his way was approached by a hobo in search of a handout. Wells gave him one of his turkey sandwiches, and as he resumed his walk he heard the yard phone ringing in the distance. He paused, and nearly walked on, figuring that the call would have nothing to do with him. But he returned to the phone box, picked up the receiver, and heard his friend explain that he had changed his mind, and was, literally, clearing the track back to Chippewa Falls.

The Wells home was close to the track; and, sitting at his bedroom window, Wells's son Floyd could see far down the line. When he spotted the dot of a headlight in the distance he shouted downstairs to his mom, who cautioned him that it was too early for Dad's train. But she was mistaken. It was indeed his dad's train, barreling down the track like a greyhound. Floyd ran out of the house and into the nearby yard just in time to see his

It's 6:45 AM, and a hardworking Milwaukee Road commuter train, named the Cannonball, is picking up a few passengers at Watertown Junction, Wisconsin, en route to Milwaukee. A Christmas wreath decorates one of the station's windows. Artist Gil Reid dated his picture at around 1950.

GIL REID

dad climbing down from his panting engine. F. E. smiled at his son and said, "Hi." It was still a few minutes to Christmas day.

Wells and his crew would have sympathized with an unnamed brakeman's peril one Christmas Eve, described in *I Travel by Train* by Rollo Walter Brown. The man had somehow become trapped between two cars on a freight train that was slowly gathering speed. Brown quoted the man's colorful account: "Can you imagine what it's like . . . slipping down, ka plump, between two flat cars when they're moving? I did that once starting on a night run to Omaha. I had sense enough to keep running down there between the two sets of trucks, but she was already going too fast for me to dodge out across the rails, and I didn't know how long I was going to be able to keep on running, with the engine picking up a little all the time. Then she began to slow down and finally stopped! Boy oh boy! The engineer said his engine didn't feel as if she was pulling just right, and he thought he'd better stop and find out what was wrong before he got going. Now isn't that good enough for a book?" Brown readily agreed that it was.

On Christmas day in 1952 George Ellert, a road foreman of engines for the New York Central, had a similar close call with a moving train, in this case the Twentieth Century Limited, an extra-fare express that no one, least of all a Central employee, would dare delay. "One Christmas day," Ellert wrote, "I was running a suburban train out of Chicago to Chesterton, Indiana, that left forty minutes before the Century. You always tried to beat the Century to Porter, Indiana, to get on the siding. Well, we had a stop at Dune Park to let passengers off. It was below freezing, about ten degrees below zero, and the reverse gear froze up on the engine I was running, so I had to get out on the running gear. And here was the Century right on my tail. So I got to Chesterton, got on the siding, and heard the dispatcher calling right away: 'Why did you delay the Century on Christmas day?'"

The plight of Barry Anderson, a fireman on the Southern Pacific in 1955, had nothing to do with getting out of the way of moving trains. He was concerned that he wouldn't have any work at all on Christmas day because

OPPOSITE The hard work attending holiday travel was nowhere more emphatically exemplified than in Buffalo, New York, a city famous for paralyzing lake-effect snow storms. Central Station, completed in 1929, stands imposingly just three miles east of Lake Erie in this photograph taken by Ed Nowak, a New York Central company photographer from 1941 to 1967.

Wishing Papa a
Merry Christmas.

Lake Shore & Michigan Southern Ry.

Pre-eminent in perfectness of roadbed, track adjustment, equipment, and in safety, comfort and certainty of service. The Lake Shore & Michigan Southern Railway affords the most perfect travel facilities that can be obtained.

We have issued a neat miniature calendar for 1901 for home use, being a direct reproduction, by color photography, from the original of one of George Taggart's delightful paintings; subject : "After a Long Silence." This will be sent to any address for four cents in postage, by A. J. SMITH, G.P.&T.A., Cleveland, O.

Waving to the engineer of a passing train is almost instinctive, especially in youngsters. How much more exciting it must have been to wave to Dad, even if he was working on Christmas. This ad ran in the December 1900 issue of the *Cosmopolitan* magazine.

OPPOSITE A long Pittsburgh & Lake Erie freight crosses the Ohio River bridge at Beaver Station, Pennsylvania, about twenty miles north of Pittsburgh. Two yard workers take a break from decorating a tree to greet the train's engineer. The year is 1949, and the artist is Howard Fogg.

of his low seniority. Still, he hoped that firemen with more seniority would want to take time off for the holiday; and three days before Christmas he got a call to fire a steam engine dragging a freight out of the San Francisco Bayshore yard across the bay to Tracy, a town eighty-two miles southeast of the Bayshore terminal. He recalled that he did yearn a bit for Christmas at home as his train passed trackside dwellings decked out with bright holiday decorations. On Christmas day he was back at work, however, this time deadheading out of Tracy on the Owl, an overnight passenger train from Los Angeles en route to Oakland, where Anderson would steer another freight back to San Francisco.

A year later, diesels had replaced all the steam engines on the SP's coast division. Anderson had seen it coming, of course, and was proud that he'd been able to fire the last of the magnificent steamers, even if it had meant spending the hours of Christmas Eve and Christmas day shoveling coal and watching the steam-pressure gauge. For years he felt that Christmas 1955 was one of the most memorable holidays he'd ever celebrated.

The Pittsburgh & Lake Erie Railroad locomotive shop in McKees Rocks, Pennsylvania. Howard Fogg created a scene that few passengers ever saw—late-night railroad-yard activity complete with a sparkling Christmas tree.

Another Christmas work order was assigned in 1969 to Michael Garvey, a brakeman on the Chicago, Burlington & Quincy Railroad. Garvey had no way of knowing that this particular shift would be blessed by a real-life Christmas angel. He and his crew were scheduled for a Christmas Eve run from North Kansas City, Missouri, to Mexico, Missouri, where they would spend the night and return home late on Christmas day. They slept in on Christmas morning, then set out for their favorite restaurant, intent on celebrating the day as best they could. But the restaurant was closed for the holiday, as was every other eating place in the small town. They trudged back to their motel, and explained their plight to the desk clerk.

The gloom was disspelled quickly, however, when the clerk told the men that she'd just gotten a call from a woman wondering if any delayed or stranded travelers would enjoy a home-cooked Christmas dinner. The woman had prepared dinner for her daughter's family, who, at just about the last minute, had called and said they couldn't make the trip. "Can't let this good food go to waste," she told the trainmen after they had trooped across town to her home. She ushered them into a large dining room, in the center of which a candlelit table fairly sagged beneath the weight of a huge, butter-browned turkey, bowls of dressing and mashed potatoes, gravy, green beans, cranberries, nuts, and oranges.

Everyone sat down, and the hostess said grace, to which the men added a hearty "amen." Garvey remembers a sumptuous meal, made unforgettable by the woman's natural generosity, and her role in restoring the joy of the day. Sustenance, cheer, and conversation continued until mid-afternoon, when Garvey reluctantly mentioned that it was time to get back to work. The woman offered a package of leftovers, a gift gladly accepted. As the men stood in the foyer putting on their coats, the phone in the kitchen rang. While the woman took the call, Garvey beckoned to his crew to follow him back into the dining room. He placed a five-dollar bill next to his plate, and his four companions followed suit. They all waved to the woman as they left, happy for her distraction since they knew she would be adamant about not accepting the money. Each man felt that the "sharing of a caring stranger," as Garvey put it, was beyond price.

Railroad people returned such generosity abundantly. Norman Sevy, a brakeman on a Southern Pacific freight train stalled in the grip of a northern Nevada Christmas Eve blizzard in 1960 shared some Christmas cheer with an unexpected guest. He was sitting in the caboose, warding off the minus-twenty-degree cold seeping into the stove-warmed car when he heard a voice outside shout, "Hey, in the caboose!" Sevy cracked open the door and saw a man wrapped in an Army surplus coat, wearing a knit cap pulled down over his ears, his beard and eyebrows coated with frost. The

Jones was a Southern Pacific agent in Yuma, Arizona. His affectionate parody appeared in the *S. P. Bulletin* in December 1952.

OPPOSITE A public-relations greeting by the Association of American Railroads in the late 1940s.

RAILROAD CHRISTMAS STORY
[by R.F. JONES]

 was the night before Christmas on the Southern Pacific
The rush was all over, on business terrific.
The passengers slept, each in his bed;
The reefers were spotted at the door of each shed.
The rip track was empty, the team tracks were full,
The very last switcher had made its last pull,
When out on the drill arose such a clatter,
The yardmaster jumped to see what's the matter.
And what to wondering eyes did appear,
But an unscheduled extra with a flock or reindeer!
He knew in a flash—his mind was so quick—
That the worried conductor was good old Saint Nick.
It seemed that a drawbar had pulled from the sleigh.
And the special was sure to incur a delay.
But quick as a wink the whole yard got busy
At fixing things up at a speed that was dizzy.
The carmen swarmed out, the brakemen fell to,
The switchmen joined in, and the whole roundhouse crew.
And so in a trice the trouble was cleared.
Saint Nick was amazed as he stroked his white beard.
Before you would know it he got the high sign,
He got a clear board and was on the main line.
And the last that was heard as his markers showed bright,
Was "Merry Christmas to all and to all a good night!"

man had been riding in a freight car ten cars up from the caboose. When he asked how long the train might be delayed, Sevy told him that it might be a while, and invited him into the caboose. He asked the traveler where he was headed, and was told simply, "to the end of the snow."

Earlier that day, Sevy and his family had enjoyed a Christmas Eve dinner, and he had brought along a feast of leftovers wrapped in aluminum foil

and stuffed into Tupperware containers. Sevy invited his guest to join him for a late-night supper. The man hesitated at first, then opened his pack and took out a can of pork and beans, which he offered to share with his host. Sevy understood the point of pride. He told his companion that pork and beans were just the right touch to round out the banquet. Minutes later the pork and beans joined Sevy's mix of turkey, sage dressing, sweet potatoes, and gravy on top of the pot-bellied stove; and as the meal simmered, the caboose was filled with a delicious aroma. By the time the men began eating, it was a few minutes past midnight. Both agreed that it was a proper Christmas, after all.

Soon after the wayfarer returned to his freight-car hideaway, the conductor swung aboard the caboose, announcing that the train was finally ready to resume its westward progress. He spotted the empty can of pork and beans and asked about it. Sevy said that it was his Christmas dinner. The conductor grunted: "Some Christmas dinner." "Yes," Sevy thought, "a real Christmas dinner."

In the late 1930s, the Kansas City Southern Lines issued an abridged version of Dickens's *A Christmas Carol* to its friends and customers.

OPPOSITE Howard Fogg placed many of his matchless paintings in holiday settings. The scene here is the Gateway Yard in Youngstown, Ohio. A Pittsburgh & Lake Erie freight passing over the bridge carries a gondola stuffed with Christmas trees, and wreaths decorate a yard pole and office windows.

Under ordinary circumstances, the engineer of a hardworking locomotive would have no time for acts of holiday goodness. But Margaret Betts's grandfather, a Canadian Pacific engineer working out of Halifax, Nova Scotia, during the 1930s, devised an annual ritual for dispensing Christmas gifts while traveling at full speed. Betts's memoir concerns oranges, and her grandfather's allergy to them. He could barely touch them without exhibiting a reaction, never mind eat them or drink the juice—except, for some mysterious reason, at Christmas. On Christmas day he would miraculously suspend his aversion, and lug a large bag of oranges aboard his engine. Wearing a wide grin he would wave to his family, tug on the whistle cord, and throttle into the night. Betts was always left wondering how a serious allergy could disappear on a train at Christmas.

A few years later, after her family moved to Massachusetts, she learned what became of all those oranges, and why her grandfather had toted them along at Christmas time. She was hospitalized with a broken leg several

The Phoebe Snow, traveling daily between New York and Chicago, via the Poconos and Buffalo, was the pride of the Lackawanna Railroad. It is seen here in Binghamton, New York, just a few days before Christmas in 1956, waiting for a heavily laden cart of holiday packages and mail to be wheeled up to the U.S. Postal Service car.

days before Christmas, and a nurse, hoping to distract the teenager from the hospital gloom, told her stories of her childhood in Halifax, Nova Scotia. Betts was fascinated by the coincidence and listened raptly to the nurse's stories. She related that her family had been very poor throughout the Depression years, and that during the winter she and her brothers and sisters would walk along the railroad tracks near their home, picking up lumps of coal that had fallen from passing trains. An engineer on one of the trains, she recalled with a smile, was very special. He would order his fireman to fling shovels full of coal in front of the children, which were retrieved gratefully and stuffed into burlap sacks. At this point, the nurse drew closer to her patient and told of how that same engineer would, at Christmas time, include with the precious

"My work is done, the morning sun
Will bring the joy of Christmas fun,
And then because," sighs Santa Claus.
"Its tolerance the world withdraws.
I'm only here but once a year,
And after that I disappear.
But you bestow, sweet Phoebe Snow,
A daily joy on those who go.
Like you in trains where travel stains
Are seldom seen, and that explains
Why I believe that Christmas Eve
Can see no joy that I may leave,
That equals quite in real delight,
The joy you give with Anthracite."

A holiday poem from a Lackawanna Railroad ad in the December 25, 1906, edition of the *New York Times*. The Phoebe Snow was the Lackawanna's elite train running between New York and Buffalo. A young woman dressed in white, also named Phoebe Snow, appeared in most of the ads, touting the carrier's use of anthracite, which produced less smoke.

supplies of coal, dozens of oranges. "Oranges all along the tracks," she remembered. "Gleaming brightly amid the black lumps of coal. I will never forget it. To us, Christmas was the sight of oranges in the snow."

Despite the clatter of sleet against the window, and the prospect of spending Christmas in a hospital bed, Betts felt a warm glow. She had learned the whole story of how her grandfather had transformed an allergy into a blessing.

Another engineer, this one running the Santa Fe Chief in southern California during the early 1950s, made an unscheduled stop in Duarte on Christmas day in 1953, to deliver gifts from himself and the crew to Jill Miller, an eighteen-year-old suffering from rheumatic fever. She would sit on her porch during good weather, or next to her bedroom window at other

Last December, as the Christmas season approached, there was a general feeling of humbug in my heart. Nevertheless, one afternoon I dutifully climbed the stairs to the attic to get the Christmas tree and decorations. While rummaging around in the attic, I found a large model-train-set box—and I remembered my father.

He loved trains. The real ones, that is, twelve-inches-to-the foot. The ones that shook the ground when you stood close; smelled of creosote, soot, grease, and diesel oil; that cleared the way through a foggy consciousness with its piercing scream and caused you to dream, or woke you from them in the night sounding of far-off places. Oh yes, he loved trains.

And it showed. From our house beside the Chicago, Burlington & Quincy tracks in Palmyra, Missouri, he could hear them coming. He would race to the fence in the front yard and watch them pass, giving them a running inspection, waving a greeting to the trainmen—absorbed in the moment and the romance of it all. When the weather was bad he would do the same from our front-room window. He loved trains. Freight trains or Zephys, it didn't matter—he loved them all. For him there were always the trains.

Sometimes he would observe something amiss—dragging equipment, a shifted load, or a bearing glowing red from the increased friction of an inadequately lubricated journal box. When he did he would call the local station agent or the dispatcher in Hannibal, who would relay the information to the train. Once he spotted fire flying from locked wheels skidding on the rails beneath a wooden boxcar. Realizing there was imminent danger and no time to relay information, he jumped into his car and hurriedly drove ahead of the train, flagging it down

at a place called Woodland, some five miles away. Both trainmen and officials were grateful for his friendship and for the extra pair of eyes looking after their safety. He became known to them all affectionately as "The Mailman," for he was the postmaster of our small town.

I cradled the box in my hands and slowly opened the lid to look inside. The contents were familiar from my youth. It was all there, the locomotive, the cars, the caboose, the track—each laying in a special cutout having lovingly been put away many years ago. Carefully I lifted the locomotive from its resting place. I turned it over and over, admiring it anew, and felt contentment as I caressed the memento. As I was placing the locomotive back into the box, I saw a small tag lying in the bottom of its cutout. I picked it up and read the works, "To the mailman and his children, from the trainmen of BRT Local 19, Christmas 1964"—and I remembered the story.

Although I was but two months old that Christmas, it has since become a part of our family's lore. My father, Corbyn Jacobs, was working in the post office the Thursday afternoon of December 24, 1964, when, about 4:00 PM, he received a phone call from the local station agent.

"Corbyn," he said, "this is the CB&Q station agent. The rear end of Kansas City-to-Chicago eastbound manifest freight 74 will be stopping at your house this afternoon about 4:30 PM. We would like you and your children to be there to meet it. We have called the local newspaper and they are sending someone out to take pictures."

"What's going on?" asked my dad.

"Santa Claus is coming to town," replied the agent.

So my father came home early that day, put coats and

THE GHOST
OF A CHRISTMAS
PRESENT
✦
John C. Jacobs,
as told to John A. Swearingen

mittens on my older sister, Julie, five, and brother, Jody, two, then took them outside to stand in the front yard to await the arrival of 74. Shortly after 4:30, as a lavender dusk was descending, a headlight appeared in the west which grew larger as it approached. In the gathering darkness only shapes, not colors, could be seen. But as it neared our yard the headlight brightly illuminated the red nose of one of a quartet of GP20s.

Horns blowing, lights flashing, exhaust cracking, motors whining, ground shaking, faces smiling, arms waving, they passed my father, sister, and brother in a great display of festive spirit. As the end of the train approached, it slowed, then stopped. The light inside the waycar shined brightly as the back door opened. The rear-end crewmen, conductor Marion "Dutch" Whitworth, and brakeman Jack Murphy, descended the steps carrying a small envelope and a Christmas present wrapped in bright red paper. Joyous smiles, greetings, glad-handing, and laughter ensued as they met my father, sister, and brother. "Merry Christmas, to you all," said Whitworth, handing the presents to my father, then kneeling down to cuddle Julie and Jody.

Murphy shook hands with my father. "Corbyn," he said, "The Brotherhood of Railroad Trainmen Local 19 at Brookfield took up a collection this year to buy Christmas presents for our No. 1 fan. When we told the railroad officials what we were doing they were behind us all the way—readily granted us permission to stop here today. Everyone with the railroad very much appreciates your friendship and all you do for us."

My father never forgot that afternoon and told the story often. He recounted, too, how the week after that Christmas we made a "thank you" sign and placed it in our yard so the trainmen of BRT Local 19 would see our gratitude.

The presents were an S-gauge train set for the children and twenty dollars for my father. I remember the many hours my sister, brother, father, and I enjoyed play-

ing with the train. But as years passed it was gradually ignored, then forgotten and put away by my father until I found it in the attic last December.

I put the small tag and locomotive back into the box, then reverently closed the lid. I gently tucked the box under my arm and gathered up the tree and decorations. I left the attic, and as I descended the stairs a warm feeling of Christmas filled my heart, experiencing the joy the gift was still giving—the joy of fellowship and gratitude.

When I got to the living room I went over to my father, who was sitting in his easy chair looking out the front-room window, and showed it to him. His face brightened and his eyes glowed, as his children's did on that Christmas Eve afternoon many years ago when Santa Claus, disguised as the Chicago, Burlington & Quincy Railroad, stopped in our front yard.

It is said by some that "the Q's" style was to pinch pennies, figuring the dollars would take care of themselves. Maybe the railroad was as parsimonious as Scrooge, but it should always be said that once in the Christmas season of 1964, it knew how to keep Christmas well. Oh yes, very well indeed!

times, and wave faithfully to passing Santa Fe trains. Still another engineer stopped his Illinois Central freight in front of the Miller sister's home on December 20, 1949, to dispense gifts in appreciation of the little girls' daily greetings to IC freight and passenger trains. Stopping a through train to bestow gifts to little girls is a bit like halting an ocean liner to toss a token to a fisherman in response to a friendly wave; but railroad men are as sentimental as they are dedicated, and they thought nothing of small delays to perform kind acts.

On a larger scale, the New York Central management decided in 1943 to send Christmas gift boxes to each of its 26,000 employees serving in the armed forces. Unfortunately, the source of this story failed to specify what was in the boxes, but a good guess might be warm socks or something special to eat, to counteract the monotony of service chow.

The Christmas season generally brings out the best in everyone, but since the railroads and their people figured so prominently in day-to-day living during the first half of the twentieth century, stories of kind acts by railroaders took on mythic proportions. On the preceding pages is an account of a grand gesture made by some crewmen working a Chicago, Burlington & Quincy freight train on Christmas Eve in 1964. The author is the beneficiary's son, recounting the event nearly thirty-five years later.

As recently as 2003 the tradition of railroad generosity was alive and well, thanks to the Canadian National's fifth annual Holiday Trains campaign. Two trains, their engines and cars decorated with hundreds of lights, offer live nightly musical performances from boxcar stages. The train travels from Montreal to Vancouver, and a U.S. counterpart covers CPR's Delaware & Hudson route from Scranton, Pennsylvania, into New York State, then into southern Ontario, and finally on to Portal, North Dakota, via Chicago over the CPR's SOO Line. In the four years prior to 2003, the trains have raised over $1 million, and collected more than 160 tons of food for hunger relief along their routes.

A Happy Holiday Season

FROM THE MEN AND WOMEN OF THE

BALTIMORE & OHIO RAILROAD

Of all the pleasures of childhood, none matched the joy of waking up on Christmas morning, tiptoeing into the living room, and discovering an electric train set up beneath the tree. This moment marked the end of weeks of agonized anticipation, as well as a cessation of mysterious activities by parents intent on hiding packages from inquisitive children. As a matter of fact, the anticipation was nearly as delicious as the culmination. Before the unwrapping it was possible to imagine a truly magnificent layout, complete with the newest accessories and rolling stock. Such reveries were nourished by the gaudy catalogs put out by Lionel and American Flyer, and displays in shop windows and in the toy sections of department stores. During the first half of the twentieth century, a toy electric train was the centerpiece of most youngsters' Christmas celebrations. Generations later, memories of trains

OPPOSITE In this scene painted by Doug Hart, a youngster is indicating exactly what he hopes to find under this Christmas tree.

on Christmas morning are still recalled with loving detail.

Bill Purdom, an artist currently living in Wilmington, North Carolina, remembers vividly Christmas 1956, when his family was living in Wyoming, Pennsylvania. During December he and his younger brother were forbidden to enter the cellar, from which the sounds of saws and hammers were heard after supper and on the weekends leading up to Christmas day. On Christmas morning the boys finally were invited to come down to the cellar. At first they saw only a four-by-eight-foot sheet of plywood hanging close to the ceiling. Then their dad activated a pulley mechanism and the sheet began to slowly descend: a moment later, the boys gasped at the sight of an American Flyer train panorama, with buildings, accessories, grass, trees, and an engine puffing wisps of smoke as it circled the layout, tugging a string of freight cars. It was, Bill later recalled, "the most magical Christmas ever."

John Huster's memories came flooding back in 1988, shortly after his father died. Among his father's files and papers Huster found some pictures taken on Christmas day thirty years earlier. The pictures recalled his discovery that day of a large, gift-wrapped carton under the tree with his name on it. He remembers that he wasn't especially excited. "I figured it was a new winter jacket, or snow pants, or some other necessary item kids are afflicted with on Christmas mornings," he wrote, expressing the sentiments of most six-year-olds. Instead, he unwrapped a blue-and-yellow box containing an American Flyer Keystone Rocket Freight, consisting of a Pennsylvania switch engine, a rocket-launcher car, a floodlight car, and a yellow caboose. John was dumbfounded. He never imagined that his parents could afford such a gift. He learned later that his mother had saved S&H Green Stamps for almost a year in order to get it for him. Later that morning, John was taken downstairs to the basement where his father was attaching legs to a four-by-eight sheet of plywood. The table soon became a proper stage for the precious gift.

A year later, thanks to the American Flyer catalog, John was lulling him-

GILBERT TOYS   *American Flyer Trains*

1951

SANTA FE

325

ERECTOR · CHEMISTRY · ATOMIC ENERGY · MAGIC · MICROSCOPE · TOOLS · PUZZLES

self to sleep with visions of a railroad empire. In fact, it took several years to assemble even a modestly equipped layout. Two items—a dual control transformer and a whistling billboard—eluded him until 1983. He was then, as he put it, "a thirty-one-year-old kid . . . finally completing my childhood shopping list."

Another family memoir, this one spanning seventy years, was recounted by Hal Hensler, a middle-school principal from Rolling Hills Estates in California. Hensler's father received an American Flyer passenger train set for Christmas in 1927. For several years thereafter he lovingly polished the engine and cars at the close of the holiday season, and put them back in their original boxes. A period of years followed during which the set

The 1951 American Flyer catalog. Such publications ushered in the Christmas-wish season for millions of youngsters.

remained safely stored away, and then in 1956 the old train was brought out again. That Christmas, Hal's older brother got an American Flyer Santa Fe "Chief" set, and as a consolation Hal was offered his father's set to play with. "I had a wonderful time bouncing back and forth between the train sets and sharing the magic that Dad obviously felt as a ten-year-old," Hensler wrote.

His son's devotions prompted the senior Hensler to take his antique set to a hobby shop, in hopes of trading it for some new American Flyer equipment. The set turned out to be worth three sets of new trains, plus enough accessories, switches, and controls to launch a year-around hobby. For forty years Hensler's dad added to his basement empire, patronizing the same hobby shop and befriending the proprietor, Doug DuBay. When he moved to California, Mr. Hensler kept in touch with DuBay, for a while by phone and letter, and then only via the dealer's ads in *Classic Toy Trains* magazine.

A Christmas still life: dolls, ribbons, Santa on skis, and a selection of American Flyer trains and accessories are in evidence. American Flyer was always a faltering second to Lionel in the toy-train competition; but there were many who stoutly defended the line, and many who now collect and recollect the sort of precious antique items seen here.

OPPOSITE The father-son bond was a recurring theme in Lionel advertising. This early-1950s scene does include Mom, but only in an approving role, as the copy indicates. The family pet seems set on disrupting the Christmas harmony.

In 1997 the senior Hensler read that DuBay's collection was being put up for auction. He called the Stout Auction company, got Greg Stout on the phone, and learned that his set was still in the collection, and would be part of the sale. Hensler told Stout the story behind the steam locomotive and trio of passenger cars, and Stout suggested that he place a bid. Hensler did so, and after a suspenseful wait, Stout called with the news that Hensler's bid had won. He added that the vying bidders had dropped out of the competition when they were told the story of the set's provenance. Three weeks before Christmas, Hensler Senior opened his front door to a UPS driver, who delivered a sturdy carton containing the American Flyer train set the eighty-year-old gentleman had cherished seven decades before.

The theme of father and son bonding flavors many Christmas toy-train memoirs. Print advertisements and train catalogs invariably depicted fathers and sons busily absorbed with train sets. Mothers and sisters were occasionally sighted, but always in the background, playing cheerleader roles.

Lionel Trains make a Boy feel like a Man

and a Man feel like a Boy

Everybody is Happy when it's a Lionel Train Christmas

Everybody gets into the act, especially when it's Lionel Trains for Christmas.

Sonny dreams of himself in a snappy engineer's cap, hand at the throttle of a 500-ton mainliner... thundering ahead, real whistle a-blowing, real smoke a-puffin'. Yes, sonny is thrilled with power and responsibility. He is a man among men, a man to be envied — a Lionel engineer.

And say, Dad; who got these trains for Christmas? You're acting like a boy. You'll show him how to run these trains, eh! You had Lionel Trains when you were a kid. Well, it's great to feel like a kid again, Dad, and it's good for you. For proof, just look at that gleam in Mom's eyes.

And remember, only Lionel Trains match a boy's Christmas dream, and Dad's too. The world's finest trains for over 50 years, they are unequaled for scale — detailed railroad realism, for steel wheeled solidity ... for remote control precision ... for the thrill, speed, power, climb and control that only Magne-Traction* gives you. See catalogue at your dealer's or send coupon for special offer.

Available in "0" gauge sets and in most "027" sets.

Send coupon for 36-page Lionel catalogue plus R. R. sound effects record plus 10 billboards.

Plays on all 78 RPM phonographs except some spindle or automatic changers.

During the 1940s and 1950s, political correctness was not even conceived of. We believed that girls preferred dolls and that boys were supposed to play with trains. It is not a nostalgic impression that those were simpler times; it is a fact. Another father-son toy-train ritual involved Dad's usurpation of the Christmas layout, to the dismay of Junior, who is pictured watching disconsolately while Dad monopolizes the transformer controls. But there was never a role for Mom or Sis.

Bill Kierce's father, however, was not in a position to dominate his son's train set, nor was he even able to arrange it beneath the Christmas tree. The set, a Buddy "L" steam engine with tender, boxcar, gondola, flatcar, and caboose, was a garden-scale outfit, meant for outdoor play, and too big for any indoor locale short of a ballroom. The engine was more than two feet long and almost a foot high, and weighed thirty-one pounds. It was sturdy enough to sit on, which is what seven-year-old Bill did that Christmas morning in 1927.

But just sitting on the engine quickly grew monotonous, and as soon as the weather moderated, Bill's dad arranged a layout in the backyard, set

A time-honored Christmas-morning scene showed Dad taking control of the train set, much to the dismay of his young son. The ritual is taken here to new heights of control and dismay by artist John Held, Jr., in a drawing that appeared in the December 19, 1931, issue of *Liberty* magazine.

on a two-foot-high trestle to avoid grading a path around the lawn's perimeter. Because the train was not powered, the trestle was built slightly higher at the start than at the end, which enabled the train to roll by itself from the top to a bumper block at the finish. Bill would trot alongside, holding one of the cars gently to keep the train from gaining too much speed. Then one day during a routine journey, disaster struck. Halfway through the tour Bill tripped over one of the trestle braces, lost his grip on the train, and fell. He watched, his eyes filling with tears, as his train gathered speed and rolled unimpeded toward the bumper.

The collision was all too realistic, Bill recollected. The engine smashed into the bumper, flew off the trestle, and gouged up a two-foot chunk of turf on the lawn. The tender tore the coupler off the flatcar, but the rest of the train remained precariously on the trestle, jackknifed and derailed. Bill's wails brought dad to the rescue. The engine had suffered a badly twisted pilot, a crushed bell bracket, and several bent handrails. Bill's dad straightened the pilot, repaired the bell bracket, realigned the handrails, and set the locomotive and tender back on the trestle. The train was soon rolling again, but a seven-year-old can be unforgiving. He wrote that the train was never again the same for him.

Another toy-train crisis, this one suffered by John and Louis Zollo of Brooklyn, New York, on Christmas day in 1932, was not alleviated by their dad, but by their seventeen-year-old aunt. The boys, ages five and three, received a Lionel freight-train set, complete with a copper-plated tunnel, as a joint gift. But their delight quickly palled when they discovered that a transformer had been accidentally omitted from the carton. No train ran beneath the Zollo Christmas tree that morning.

But early the next morning the boys' teenage aunt set out for Macy's, carrying the incomplete set, and accompanied by little John, for whom a subway trip to Manhattan was an epic adventure. The store, John recalled, was a madhouse. Undaunted, his aunt grabbed Bill's hand and plunged into the crowd surrounding the toy counter. She explained to a thoroughly

The cover of Lionel's fiftieth-anniversary catalog featured the company's Magne-Traction feature, and a glimpse of a sturdy Hudson 4-6-4 steam locomotive. Magne-Traction depended as much on weight as it did on the imagination, but the concept helped sell a lot of trains.

addled clerk that the transformer was missing from the boys' new train set. In the confusion the clerk misunderstood and handed over another entire set—this one including the transformer—without asking for the return of the first set. By nightfall there were two trains speeding beneath the Zollos' Christmas tree; and, more than sixty years later, John's train set was still running, now part of a layout that he built for his grandson.

Grandfathers have as much fun as fathers with toy trains, maybe more. Joe Jesensky, writing in the December 1995 issue of *Classic Toy Trains*, recalled his grandfather's involvement in a good-natured family deception played out on Christmas Eve in 1950. It was the custom in Joe's family to open gifts on Christmas Eve, but as the evening wore on after dinner, there was

1950

LIONEL SCOUT TRAIN $14.95

"Columbia" 2-4-2 die-cast Locomotive —
Equipped with Lionel Magne-Traction —
3 accurately-detailed freight cars

SET INCLUDES 25 WATT
TRANSFORMER. Lionel No.
1011 transformer has continu-
ous voltage control — ample
power output for train and
several accessories. Handsome,
durable case with grip style
handle which gives finger-tip
control of your train.

MANUMATIC TRACK SECTION
Uncouples cars like magic! Just
press the lever to cut loose any
car from the train. To recouple
merely back train into the standing car. Section can be placed
anywhere on the track.

No. 1113

No. 1113
LIONEL SCOUT 3-CAR FREIGHT

Without doubt the most beautifully scaled, most complete model train at this amazingly low price of $14.95!
Look closely at this sturdy locomotive modified copy of
the "Columbia" 2-4-2 type used on the big roads. Cars,
scale-detailed as only Lionel can do it, are mounted on
die-cast trucks with solid steel wheels. Manumatic track
section permits you to uncouple these cars without even
touching them. Set is 3 ft., 5 ins. long. Track forms oval
37⅝" x 27⅝". Transformer included.

Lionel No. 1113 3-Car "Scout" Set Comprises:

1 No. 1120 Steam-type Locomotive
1 No. 1001T Enamel Finish Steel Tender
1 No. 1002 Gondola Car
1 No. 1005 Single Dome "Sunoco" Oil Car
1 No. 1007 Caboose
8 sec. 1013 Curved Track
1 sec. 1018 Straight Track
1 No. 1009 "Manumatic" Track Section
1011 25 Watt Transformer, CTC Lockon
Tube of Lubricant, Instruction Booklet

$14.95

FOR AN ADDITIONAL $32.19 — A COMPLETE RAILROAD SYSTEM!

The layout shown here is not sold
as a unit. It is just a suggestion
as to how you can put together a
complete railroad empire of your
own — economically. Your Lionel
dealer has all the necessary track,
switches and accessories. You can
buy them all at once or individu-
ally, as your pocketbook dictates.

OVERALL DIMENSIONS:
72" by 36"

Yes, you can have a complete railroad system like
this—long stretches of track, switches, whistling station, automatic gateman, flashing highway signal,
water tower—all the excitement of big-time railroading for only $32.19 worth of equipment added
to your "Scout" set.
Illustration shows only one way of expanding your
original set. Maybe you will want to use more or
less in the way of track and accessories. The point is
—starting with the low-priced "Scout" you can build
a model railroad empire at a very moderate price.
Look it over. Discuss it with your Lionel dealer.
Here are the components of the layout shown at left:

93 Water Tower	$ 1.75
125 Whistling Station	4.95
145 Automatic Gateman	5.95
256 Freight Shed	4.50
154 Flashing Signal	4.75
309 Yard Set	.79
310 Billboard Set	1.00
1 pr. Manual Switches	4.75
2 sec. Curved Track*	.50
13 sec. Straight Track**	3.25
	$32.19

*Layout calls for 10 sec.— Scout set
includes 8.
**Layout calls for 15 sec.— Scout set
includes 1 Straight, 1 Manumatic.
Total cost of layout
(Track, switches &
accessories) $32.19
Cost of "Scout" set .. 14.95
Complete R.R. System $47.14

no sign of Santa's bounty, and Joe was beginning to lose hope. Not even Bing Crosby and the Andrews Sisters caroling from the phonograph could lift his spirits. Then his grandpa asked him to help with a chore, and Joe moodily followed him upstairs. He could not recall the nature of the errand, but he did remember his father calling out a few minutes later, announcing that Santa had arrived and was just leaving. Joe raced back downstairs, ran to the front door, flung it open, and stared out into the cold night, hoping for at least a glimpse of Santa and his reindeer. The disappointment he felt was soon erased by what awaited him in the living room: a pile of brightly wrapped packages, and a steam locomotive pulling two freight cars and a red caboose around the Christmas tree. The train was a gift from

The Lionel Scout Train that captivated Joe Jesensky on Christmas Eve 1950, and became the nucleus of his collection. The price of $14.95 was a reasonable one to pay in 1950, but the invitation to expand the set to "a complete railroad system" would cost the family nearly $50.

Joe's grandpa, who explained that it was a Lionel No. 1113 Scout set. Years later, Joe inventoried his by-then-extensive collection and remembered that it was the little Scout set that had sparked his passion for toy trains. He remembered his grandpa. "If only Grandpa had known that small train set would inspire a lifelong avocation," he wrote. "Or perhaps, as usual, he was a step ahead of me and knew it all along".

Growing up in a northern New Jersey farm town, Curtis Katz worshiped "real" trains. To be sure, he routinely brought a piece of his American Flyer equipment to school for Friday "Show and Tell" assignments, but his toy trains couldn't match the drama generated by the Lackawanna freight and passenger trains that whistled and rumbled just a few miles from his home.

One of Curtis's favorite holiday traditions was a late December trip to Newark's Pennsylvania Station, where his parents put the family dentist and his wife aboard a Florida-bound streamliner. This enabled Curtis to glimpse his favorite locomotive, the handsome GG1 electric charger that hauled Pennsylvania Railroad trains down the main line between New York and Washington.

On one memorable occasion Curtis's dad delegated the farewells to Mom, and led Curtis down to the end of the platform, to a spot where he was pretty sure the engine would stop when the Florida train pulled in. Curtis peered excitedly down the length of the train shed and through the arched portal, and moments later saw the glow of a headlight winking through a swirling snowstorm. Soon a majestic GG1 at the head of a procession of silver coaches and Pullman cars glided into the station and ground to a stop in front of Curtis and his dad. While Curtis stared pop-eyed at the humming giant, the fireman climbed down from the cab, smiled at Curtis, and nodded toward the engine. "How'd you like to have one of those under your Christmas tree?" he asked. Curtis couldn't believe this lordly figure was actually speaking to him. His awe rendered him speechless. The fireman waved, wished Curtis and his father a happy holiday, and clambered back up to his perch.

Pennsylvania Railroad's GG1, Curtis Katz's favorite. The 200-ton electric locomotive was designed by Raymond Loewy for the New York-Washington, D. C., run. Pennsy crews called them "motors," and during the late 1950s there were 139 of them in service. This painting is by Howard Fogg.

OPPOSITE Look closely at this ad and you'll see Joe DiMaggio adding his endorsement of the Lionel product line. The Yankee Clipper was the host of a weekly television program that combined baseball tips with toy-train displays and demonstrations.

Adults were, of course, the purchasers of toy trains, if not the consumers, so it was necessary to beguile them as fully as their children. This magazine cover portrays varying moods of admiration and nostalgia, and the eternal grip small trains have on the imagination.

During the drive home Curtis daydreamed raptly of a GG1 and the words the fireman had spoken to him. "The only thing that perturbed my innocent but practical child-thought on the matter," he wrote, "was not so much that our family was Jewish and thus had no Christmas tree, but rather . . . how would I have gotten the darn thing home?"

Not even celebrities were immune to the daydreams evoked by trains big or small. Frank Sinatra and Alan Ladd collected Lionel trains; Yul Brynner preferred American Flyer. Baseball stars Joe DiMaggio and Roy Campanella were often photographed with Lionel trains, and while it's not known just how much time the Yankee Clipper actually spent with them, Campy often spoke of the layout in his basement, and the fun he and his son had with it. Jack Benny devoted a brief portion of his radio show on December 17, 1950, to a scene in which his valet, Rochester, discovers a note from Jack to Santa. The show's announcer Don Wilson began:

The Saturday Evening
POST
December 15, 1956   15¢

Chicago's War on Hit-Run Killers
The Walt Disney Story: in Color
The Deadliest Airplane Ever Made
Pro Football Comes Down to Earth

DON: *And now ladies and gentlemen let's go out to Jack Benny's home in Beverly Hills. At the moment Jack is out doing his Christmas shopping, and Rochester is just leaving to do his.*
ROCHESTER: *Oh, oh, what's this on the desk? Hmm . . . a letter in Mr. Benny's handwriting. "Dear Santa . . . Christmas is almost here and it would make me very happy if you gave me a train." Hee, hee, hee. When Mr. Benny wants a train, he wants a* train. *This letter isn't addressed to Santa* Claus. *It's addressed to Santa Fe. . . . Well, they may send him one; he's mentioned them often enough.*

In his book *All Aboard*, a lively history of the Lionel corporation, Ron Hollander reports that the Santa Fe did indeed send a train set to Jack, although not on the scale Jack preferred. The company sent Lionel's version of the Santa Fe F3 diesel, resplendent in its red, yellow, and silver war-bonnet paint scheme.

Make Him the Happiest Boy in the World this Christmas...with

the Only Train ... in the World with

MAGNE-TRACTION

THE NEW SENSATIONAL 1950 **LIONEL TRAINS**

Magne-Traction — exclusive Lionel track-gripping development—is the most amazing advance in model trains. More *speed*...top speed even around tight curves! More *climb*... up tough grades where other trains can't start! More *pull*...twice as many cars twice as fast! More *control*... split-second starts and stops. It's the grand climax to all the features that have made Lionel Trains the world's finest for 50 years...built-in remote-control whistle; real smoke (odorless, harmless); remote-control knuckle couplers; steel wheels, die-cast trucks. See these great Lionel Trains...*now priced lower than for many years past.* See Magne-Traction work! Free catalog at your dealer's or send coupon for special offer.

Look at the
JOE DIMAGGIO LIONEL CLUB HOUSE TELEVISION SHOW
EVERY SATURDAY ON NBC NETWORK
See local newspapers for time and station

SPECIAL COUPON OFFER
ALL FOR 25¢

LIONEL TRAINS, Post Office Box 446
Madison Square Station, New York 10, N. Y.
I enclose 25c. Please send me special Lionel Train Catalog offer postage prepaid.

1. The new Lionel 44-page full-color catalog.
2. The "Magic of Magne-Traction Book" with new track layouts, scenic effects, etc.
3. The Lionel "Portfolio of the 19th Century Locomotive Art Prints"—in color— suitable for framing.

Name..
Address..
City ....Zone.......State..............

Arthur Godfrey, a hugely popular radio and television star during the 1940s and 1950s, went Jack one better and had a complete set of trains delivered to his home and set up in his basement family room, courtesy of the Lionel corporation. After demonstrating a small Lionel set on his TV show in November 1953, Godfrey hinted that in return for the free plug he'd be delighted to have a layout installed in his Leesburg, Virginia, home, ostensibly for his children's enjoyment. An eight-by-sixteen-foot system was hastily designed and constructed. It included two main lines, several sidings, mountains ablaze in autumn color, elevated grades running between the mountains, a painted backdrop, boxes of rolling stock, and nearly every accessory in the Lionel catalog.

Ten days before Christmas, a three-man crew set out from New York in a rented truck containing the holiday cargo. The truck broke down on the New Jersey Turnpike, was repaired, and broke down again an hour later. The weary crew finally reached Leesburg the following morning. The directions to Godfrey's house given to the men proved unavailing, and to further frustrate matters it was discovered that no one had been given Godfrey's unlisted phone number. A storekeeper was finally convinced that the men were on a legitimate errand, and he provided directions.

Once found, Godfrey's home presented another dilemma. The only access to his basement was down a narrow circular staircase, too narrow to accommodate the four four-by-eight sections of the layout. Bill Vollheim, the crew chief, resignedly distributed hacksaws to his partners. They cut the sections in half, slicing through thick plywood, tracks, wiring, and even the model mountains. The reconstruction and assembly took until midnight to complete, during which time a heavy snowfall had accumulated. By the time Voll-

This ad appeared on the back cover of the December 1995 issue of *Classic Toy Trains* magazine. Lionel was making a strong comeback at this time, thanks to renewed interest in toy trains as well as a more enlightened management.

Guess what Santa's coming to town in this year.

THE SLEIGH AND REINDEER were a nice touch, but even Santa couldn't resist the Lionel Village Trolley Company trolley set. With red, green and gold graphics and elevated roof, the trolley is unmistakable as it travels around your Christmas setting. The illuminated interior makes it easier for Santa to check his list twice, while the other full-color passenger silhouettes take in the scenery with the help of an operating directional headlight. And it promises to be a nice, quiet Christmas thanks to the trolley's DC motor. The Lionel Village Trolley Company trolley set. Make sure it stops at your house this year. **LIONEL** *Experience the magic.*

heim and his crew were ready to go, they couldn't leave. They were tired, hungry, and snowbound.

Arthur Godfrey's radio and TV persona oozed charm and down-home wit, but in person he was often short-tempered and inhospitable. He offered the Lionel team the basement floor for the night, and ordered his cook to prepare some sandwiches "in case the men were hungry," a likely circumstance since no supper had been provided. Even the magnificent layout failed to prompt much in the way of a compliment from him. Vollheim and company expressed no admiration for the "Redhead" upon their return to the Lionel offices the following day.

For youngsters lucky enough to live near a main-line railroad, the sounds and sights of trains were transfixing. The title of this painting by Ron Hatch is *No School Tomorrow*; and it's easy to imagine this fellow on his way home from an afternoon of sledding on his new Flexible Flyer, a recent Christmas gift.

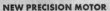

For several years thereafter, Lionel delivered a layout to Godfrey's television studio just before Christmas. The host would operate it for a few minutes, and then a Lionel spokesman would ask Godfrey if he was still enjoying his home setup. Every year Godfrey would invariably complain that the equipment was in terrible shape, and every year poor Bill Vollheim was dispatched to Leesburg to update the layout with the latest engines, cars, and accessories. It was a gesture that Lionel was happy to make, given the free publicity generated by Godfrey's program, but it was a holiday custom Vollheim came to dread.

Families that did not own TV sets, and there were a lot of them in the early 1950s, could always view toy train layouts in department stores and hobby shops. Those fortunate enough to live in or near New York City were blessed with flagship department stores, multistory train shops, and spectacular showroom layouts at Lionel's headquarters and at the Gilbert Hall of Science, where American Flyer trains paraded.

The main offices and showroom of the Lionel corporation were located on Twenty-sixth Street, just a few doors east of Fifth Avenue, in Manhattan. Display cases and shelves containing trains and equipment lined the showroom walls, but the main attraction was a sixteen-by-thirty-two-foot toy-train empire that dominated the room, and exceeded even the most extravagant childhood fantasies. Three main lines wound through tunnels, over a river, beneath an elaborate footbridge, past buildings and an imposing passenger station. Another line looped beneath the layout, appearing only at the lower level of the passenger station. Every accessory that Lionel made was on working display: a water tower, log and coal loaders, a magnetic crane, crossing gates complete with tireless, lantern-waving gatemen, a drawbridge, and more. There were sleek diesel engines and puffing

An ad from the December 5, 1931, issue of the *Saturday Evening Post*. Even as the Great Depression tightened its grip, Lionel continued to promote its trains widely, and with shameless appeals to Dad's conscience. Joshua Lionel Cowen was quoted as saying that electric trains were "the perfect instrument of father-son relationship."

OPPOSITE American Flyer hedged its bets with this ad by including space for its Erector sets and science kits. Still, the trains are in the spotlight, as is a drawing of the Gilbert Hall of Science, where a fantasy land of trains and other Gilbert toys were housed.

OPPOSITE Here are Dick and Jane, and little Sally, playing with their Christmas train, and Spot, wreaking havoc. This greeting card was distributed initially during the 1940s, and reissued in 1996 in celebration of Scott, Foresman's one-hundredth anniversary. Life-size oil paintings of Dick, Jane, and Sally still hang in the company's headquarters.

steamers, freight cars, and passenger cars. Power was delivered by four twin-levered ZW transformers, the ultimate power pack. Onlookers of all ages stood transfixed as the trains made their stately rounds, and the various accessories performed flawlessly. No one who stepped out of the elevator on the second floor of the Lionel offices ever forgot the first sight of the extravaganza. There are those who still lull themselves to sleep with images of Lionel trains endlessly traversing their routes.

Sad to say, the show could not go on forever. The display was dismantled in 1957, and might have remained just a grainy memory were it not for the vision and determination of the Jackson (Mississippi) Society of Model Engineers, and a group of volunteers from the local Ronald McDonald House. Their original idea was to create a multi-layout toy-train display in a nearby shopping mall, to be run as a fundraiser for the Ronald McDonald House. One of the volunteers, Amos McCormick, had purchased a book titled *Great Toy Train Layouts Of America*, in which the Lionel showroom layout was featured. McCormick persuaded his fellow volunteers to concentrate their resources and energies on re-creating the old Lionel display.

A painstaking quest for information followed. McCormick's research eventually produced a three-ring notebook three inches thick, stuffed with articles, photos, plans, letters, and diagrams. A sixteen-by-thirty-two-foot table, the size of the Manhattan display, was covered with exactly the same track plan and decor. Accessories and buildings were matched, and locomotives and consists were replicated. Four 250-watt ZW transformers were fastened to the control panel. Construction took almost four months, but everything was in place in time for Thanksgiving 1991, the acknowledged start of the holiday season. The display was open between Thanksgiving and New Year's Eve only, and again over the Easter and Fourth of July weekends: but during the first year, more than thirty thousand people visited, sometimes three generations at a time. McCormick happily reported that in addition to a sizeable increase in the Ronald McDonald House endowment, sales of toy trains in the area soared. He added that "visitors

Happy Holidays

All the very best from
Dick, Jane, Sally, and Spot!

ScottForesman

American Flyer ACTION ACCESSORIES

Load 'em aboard by remote control!

No. 770 BAGGAGE LOADING PLATFORM
Freight terminal realism combined with American Flyer remote control action! Here's a thrilling accessory that's all set to handle your rush rail shipments with ease—and all at the touch of a button. Die cast Packing Boxes, or Milk Cans, are placed on loading ramp. Each time control button is pressed, a box is fed singly to trainman who lowers chute extension and sends the miniature crate into the car. Accessory, which does NOT include car shown, operates ideally with No. 732 Baggage Car (illustrated) or No. 734 Box Car. Beautifully finished in realistic colors. Measures 7" long x 8½" wide x 3¾" high. Includes Milk Cans, Packing Boxes, Control Unit and Instructions.

Baggage car, shown above, is not included with No. 770 loading platform.

Cattle keep in constant motion!

No. 771 OPERATING STOCKYARD AND CAR
One of the most extraordinary accessories ever created! After switch is turned action is entirely automatic. White-faced steers in stock yard pens mill about and move continuously, some docilely, others "bucking the tide," just like real cattle. When one of the two exit gates is opened, cattle troop up ramp and into car. Stock car unloads by remote control when exit door is lined up with corral ramp.
Accessory can be operated in a variety of ways. Cattle in one pen keep moving constantly while animals in other pen are filing either into or out of car! Stock Yard has realistic corral fence; base painted grass green. Shed enameled brown with green roof. Includes Car, Stock Yard, track contact unit, twin button control, cattle and instructions.

Watch 'em troop into the car!

PLEASE REFER TO PRICE LIST

26

Two of American Flyer's most irresistible accessories—the baggage-loading platform and the operating stockyard. The ad copy was technically true: the cattle were indeed in constant motion, but often frustratingly reluctant to move in the right direction.

realized there's more to life than television and video games."

Lionel's showroom was not the only toy-train spectacular in New York during the 1950s. Just a block south of the Lionel offices, at Fifth Avenue and Twenty-fifth Street, stood the Gilbert Hall of Science, a six-story building featuring porthole windows at street level, through which tantalizing glimpses of science kits, Erector sets, and American Flyer trains tempted passers-by. The Hall was opened in the fall of 1941, predating the Lionel showroom by almost a decade. A massive train layout dominated the first floor.

Imagine a youngster entering the building with Christmas loot on his mind. He would be dazzled by steam engines puffing smoke and huffing an authentic "choo-choo" sound, timed to the motion of the drivers. Diesels wound gracefully through the scenery, occasionally emitting an air-chime whistle. Passenger cars were lit from within, with silhouettes of passengers showing through the windows. Freight cars were marked with the colors and logos of major carriers. Among the accessories were a seaboard coaler with a bucket that gulped and released quantities of play coal, a "talking" passenger station, and a baggage-loading platform that conveyed parcels down a ramp and into a waiting baggage car. The baggage car was equipped with a conveyor belt that transported the parcels to a second door where a handler flung the packages out again.

Perhaps the most remarkable accessory was the remote-controlled stock-yard and cattle car. Tiny white-faced cattle milled around two pens; and when one of the two exit gates was opened the critters trooped obediently, and sometimes not so obediently, up a ramp and into the car. When the exit door on the car was lined up with the ramp, the cattle marched back out of the car, down the ramp, and into one of the pens. While all this was going on, the herd in the adjoining pen moved back and forth and around, "some dociley; others bucking the tide," as the Flyer catalog copy put it. There was even a little shed attached to the corrals, in which you imagined the cattle might retire for the night.

A smaller train display on the second floor was available only to salesmen, buyers, and selected VIPs. The Hall remained open until 1959, outlasting the Lionel showroom by two years, at which time it was closed by edict of a consulting firm hired to restore the corporation's dwindling profits.

American Flyer trains were also on display a continent away, in the street-level windows of the Bon Marché department store in Seattle, Washington. For five Christmas seasons—1948 through 1952—a four-level layout, featuring sculpted, snow-dusted mountains, and a river and harbor with "real" water, attracted long lines of holiday shoppers. Children especially were delighted by a wiring device that slowed and stopped trains in the window, and then, after a momentary pause, sent them on their way again.

The layout's designer, Bob James, was not one to stand pat, and he altered

"Me too"

Drink
Coca-Cola

The pause
that refreshes

Hopeful children always left a
plate of cookies for Santa, and
many included a bottle of Coke
for the jolly old elf.

and augmented the system every year. In 1952 he went too far. That year the
snowy peaks and rural landscapes were replaced by skyscrapers, four-lane
highways, and a spaceport, from which an illuminated flying saucer rose, hovered and spun, and then slowly descended to its launching platform. There
were trains to be seen, but only as incidentals to the futuristic panorama.
Adults were intrigued by the display, it was reported, but kids much preferred
the traditional toy-train creations. Lines on the sidewalk were shorter that
season, and a year later there was no window display to be seen at all.

During the post–World War II decade, the rivalry between Lionel and
American Flyer reached a peak of intensity. Some of the noisiest arguments
between kids of that era focused on the following topics: Who was the best
cowboy—Roy Rogers or Gene Autry? Who was the best centerfielder—
Willie Mays, Duke Snider, or Mickey Mantle? And what was the best
model-train maker? The Lionel faithful touted the brawn and variety of
their train sets; Flyer fans derided Lionel's three-rail track and defended
what they felt were their more realistic setups. You were either a Lionel
kid or an American Flyer kid. No compromise was possible.

The companies themselves were owned and run by two singular gentlemen: Joshua Lionel Cowen, and Alfred Carlton Gilbert, better known as A.C., or, more likely, Mr. Gilbert to all but his immediate family and closest acquaintances. Born in Salem, Oregon, in 1884, Gilbert graduated from Yale in 1909 with a degree in medicine. In 1908 he won the Olympic Gold Medal in the pole-vault competition, setting a world record using a pole he invented. To the dismay of his parents he spurned a medical career; instead he formed, or joined—depending on whose account you trust— the Mysto Manufacturing Company, a producer of magic sets. In 1912 he invented the Erector set, and a year later introduced the toy at the New York and Chicago toy fairs. Its resounding success enabled Gilbert to launch the A.C. Gilbert company in 1915. In 1938 Gilbert purchased American Flyer trains from a Chicago-based company, determined to challenge Lionel's near-monopoly of the toy-train market.

Gilbert was called "The Man Who Saved Christmas," as a result of his impassioned plea in 1918 to the Council of National Defense, a wartime panel set on suspending toy sales for the holiday season. He began his oration to the council members in measured tones. "The greatest influence in the life of a boy is his toys," he said quietly, and with the sort of gender indifference typical of the time. "A boy wants fun, not education," he continued, his voice rising. "Yet through the kind of toys American toy manufacturers are turning out he gets both." At that point he paused, opened a large briefcase, took out

Despite the downturn in consumer spending brought on by the Depression, Lionel continued to advertise its trains aggressively, as seen in this ad from 1930. Note the breadth of Lionel's distribution described in the ad copy; in addition to toy and department stores, the trains could be purchased at electrical, hardware, and even sporting-goods outlets.

The Mickey and Minnie Mouse handcar was credited by some as the product that helped Lionel emerge from receivership in 1934, but it was a line of gleaming streamlined passenger trains that generated most of the recovery dollars. A year later, company owner Cowen voted himself a $10,000 bonus.

several toys, and placed one in front of each member of the committee. Moments later, curiosity surrendered to idylls of reminiscence. The stern-faced gentlemen, including the secretaries of War, Commerce, and Interior, were happily playing with tiny steam engines, model submarines, and Gilbert's signature invention, the Erector set. The Honorable Josephus Daniels, secretary of the Navy, sat on the carpeted floor of the meeting room and squinted through the submarine's periscope, imagining a German U-Boat in his sights. Christmas was rescued. Millions of children, as well as retailers, blessed Gilbert's name. A business associate added his admiration. "A.C. is something special," he said. "He's a genius of industry who chose to remain a boy."

After World War II, Gilbert aggressively fought Lionel for market share; but even in their best years, Flyer sets were outsold three to one by their rival. Gilbert retired from his company in 1954, and died in 1961. In 1967, with sales eroded by $20 million since Gilbert's death, American Flyer suffered an ignominious end: it was sold to the Lionel Corporation.

Cowen, born Joshua Lionel Cohen in 1877, was fascinated by steam engines as a youngster. Once, while trying to build one in his mother's kitchen, he touched off an

explosion that scalded his hands and blackened the walls. Undaunted, he continued tinkering, turning his mechanical aptitude to gadgets powered by electricity. In 1900 he created his first toy-train piece—a wooden gondola car with a tiny electric motor hidden beneath the floor. Named the Electric Express, the car ran around a thirty-foot circle of brass track, and was used in store windows as an attention-getter. That same year, Cowen and Harry C. Grant started a business to engage in "the manufacture of electric novelties." It was named the Lionel Manufacturing Company, and, as Ron Hollander put it, "neither childhood or Christmas would ever be the same."

Cowen did not just preside over his company; he was immersed in practically every detail of its operation. In a profile for *The New Yorker*, Robert Lewis Taylor wrote: "The chairmen of many corporation boards try to maintain a certain detachment from routine operations; Cowen, who is crazy about toy electric trains, cannot take them or leave them alone. Separated from his plant for very long, he gets jumpy and tense."

The dedication paid off. For the 1939 Christmas season, the Lionel catalog numbered fifty-two full-color pages, and was printed in a run of one million copies. Cowen ruled the world of electric trains. American Flyer was a plucky, but distant, second.

Lionel's ascendancy was not unblemished, however. The Depression, coinciding with a company banking scandal, forced the firm into receivership in 1934. But later that year, with its debts on hold, and just in time for Christmas, Lionel introduced a line of gleaming, streamlined trains, and a handcar propelled by Mickey and Minnie Mouse. The latter sold a quarter million units, and orders for 100,000 more could not be filled. Lionel's dominant market share was quickly restored. Materials shortages during World War II impacted sales, but the postwar bonanza more than compensated. By 1953, the corporation's peak year, sales topped $33 million.

As did American Flyer, Lionel began to deflate as the 1950s came to an end. By 1958, sales were down to $14.4 million. Just before Christmas of that year the eighty-one-year-old Cowen announced his retirement. A year later, with a loss of more than a million dollars reported, the firm was sold to an investment group headed by Roy Cohn, Cowen's great-nephew. Joshua Lionel Cowen died in 1965. In its obituary the *New York Herald Tribune* wrote: "The man who influenced the celebration of American Christmas almost as much as Santa Claus died yesterday."

Lionel trains lived on, surviving several shaky ownerships, until 1995, when a group of investors that included rock star Neil Young bought the line. In 2000, the centennial of Lionel trains, the new owners issued a stunning 110-page full-color catalog. Three years later the catalog had increased in size to 156 pages, and included an item that Mr. Cowen might not have appreciated. "Mr. Spiff and Puddles" is an operating accessory that includes a well-dressed gentleman, a pretty young lady, the gentleman's dalmatian dog, and a tree. When the remote-control switch is pressed the gentleman gallantly raises his hat, and his dog, standing behind him and next to the tree, raises his leg. There is evidently no water supply included, so ultimate realism is precluded, perhaps mercifully.

As devotions to toy electric trains were rekindled during the 1990s, holiday train exhibitions and excursions surged in number and popularity. Railroad museums offered Santa-accompanied train rides, and large corporations sponsored spectacular train layouts at Christmas time. One of the grandest was the Citibank Station display at the Citicorp Center in New York City. Eight railroads, all computer-controlled, operated simultaneously, and included nearly 150 items of rolling stock and locomotives running on eleven loops of track. In addition to the trains, there were numerous animated scenes featuring a woodcutter flailing away at a tree, a moving steam roller, a house under construction, and ice skaters gliding over a shim-

Holiday train exhibits proliferated early in the twenty-first century, in small towns and big, none bigger than New York. This display was on view in the New York Transit Museum Gallery Annex at Grand Central Terminal.

Few stories evoke the spirit of Christmas better than Chris Van Allsburg's book *The Polar Express*. The ride has been reenacted in dozens of locations around the country, but the most faithful version is staged annually by the Conway Scenic Railroad in New Hampshire.

mering pond. Visitors moved from a 1940s scene in Weehawken, New Jersey, past the Manhattan skyline, up the Hudson River Valley, and into the Catskill Mountains. The display was housed in a Victorian-style replica of an early-twentieth-century upstate New York depot.

Uptown from the Citicorp spectacle, the New York Botanical Garden has, since 1991, staged a holiday train show in its magnificent Edith A. Haupt Conservatory greenhouse. G-scale passenger and freight trains, pulled by a variety of steam engines and diesels, travel over 1,200 feet of track, around, between, and above lush plantings of cacti, poinsettias, and conifers. The trains pass more than one hundred New York landmarks, including the Statue of Liberty, the Apollo Theater, and the Brooklyn Bridge, all ingeniously constructed from twigs, bark, seed pods, leaves, and many other materials from nature's store. A twenty-five-foot Christmas tree, ablaze with bulbs, stands inside the entrance to the Conservatory, and holiday music sets the festive mood. Garden workers are never satisfied; the show becomes more elaborate and entertaining every year.

Children, as well as adults, who wish to ride in a train at Christmas rather than look at one, have many holiday jaunts to choose from, but none more magical than the ride staged by the Conway Scenic Railroad in New Hampshire. Inspired by Chris Van Allsburg's *The Polar Express*, the voyage reenacts the author's story of children traveling to the North Pole on a ghostly passenger train. The following article, describing a journey on the Conway Railroad, appeared in the December 1998 issue of *Yankee* magazine.

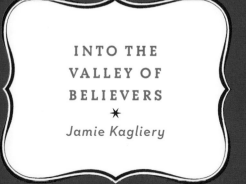

INTO THE
VALLEY OF
BELIEVERS
*
Jamie Kagliery

"Where are we going?" my mother asks. I sit wedged between her and Ian, my three-year-old son, on a bench seat made for two. Our train rocks and creaks through the New Hampshire darkness.

"The North Pole," Ian and I say at the same time.

"No, you know," she whispers now, her hand over her mouth. "I mean, which town?"

"Mom, we're heading to the North Pole." I whisper back out of the side of my mouth. "To be greeted by elves and see Santa Claus. To see him pack his sleigh and pick a child to receive the first gift of Christmas."

She sighs, sits back, and bites into a piece of candy—chocolate with a white nougat center. Ian tries to chew the entire golf-ball-sized candy and stares out the steaming-up window.

"Is it Glen?" my mother whispers again. "Bartlett? Where in this valley would they be able to build a North Pole?"

I just smile and shake my head. "Mom," I tell her, "you've got to believe."

All around us, on car No. 4 and the other cars of the Conway Scenic Railroad, children drink hot chocolate, eat candy, and stare out the windows of the train at the swiftly passing night. This train, they've heard, will take them to the North Pole to see Santa Claus, just as it took the young boy in The Polar Express.

Written and illustrated a dozen years ago by Providence, Rhode Island, resident Chris Van Allsburg, The Polar Express has become a holiday classic. It tells the story of a young boy whose friends tell him there is no Santa Claus. He refuses to believe it, and on Christmas Eve he lies in bed, listening for the sound of hooves on the roof. Instead, he hears a train's whistle. He creeps downstairs and boards the train destined for the North Pole. On the way, the boy and dozens of other children pass through dense forests and deep valleys. Wild animals scatter as they rush by. At the North Pole, Santa and the elves prepare feverishly for the trip around the world. Santa picks one child—the boy in the story—to receive the first gift of Christmas. Though he can have anything he chooses, he asks Santa for a bell from his sleigh. On the train home, the boy loses the bell through a hole in his bathrobe, only to find it again, wrapped up under the tree on Christmas morning. He loves the way it sounds, but his parents can't hear it. Only believers can hear the bell. For the rest of his life, he will hear it.

When we boarded the train at the restored turn-of-the-century station in North Conway village, we could see lights sparkling on Mount Cranmore. To Ian they looked like stars so close he could almost touch them. Inside, we sat on leather seats with curved arms; the oak paneling, the high ceilings, etched-glass doors and transoms made us feel we were traveling in another era. In the spring, summer, and fall, the trains of the Conway Scenic Railroad carry passengers on scenic tours of the Mount Washington Valley. But on December weekends, in the chill of the evening, the trains depart for only one destination: the North Pole. Some years ago, after reading Chris Van Allsburg's book, several local folks thought of using the Conway Scenic Railroad to reenact the North Pole journey. The first year, there were five trips; in 1997 there were ten, all of them sold out.

If you truly need to know where the train is going, one of the three hundred local volunteers might tell you that the train goes from Conway to Bartlett. The North Pole, if you insist, is the Bear Peak Lodge at Attitash. Every weekend evening, volunteers labor mightily to convert the lodge into the North Pole and Santa's workshop. The profits from the train rides are used to promote literacy programs in the valley. And those volunteers—ninety are needed each night—dress up as elves, complete with red velvet suits, pointy shoes, and hats with bells. The volunteers become chefs, too, who ride the trains in snow-white toques, serving hot chocolate and chocolate nougat candies.

Carolers in blue velvet come down the train aisles singing "O Christmas Tree." All around us, some children sing, most chatter. They're dressed in PolarFleece, stocking caps, pajamas, and flannel nighties. Some have teddy bears. Some are rehearsing what they will tell Santa if he asks them what they want. "I want a Barbie." I hear, and "Hot Wheels garage!" Even the grown-ups are giddy. There's jostling and hot-chocolate splashing. A little sister gets elbowed off a seat near a window, and I hear parents whispering of "time-outs."

Outside, the full moon shines on the snow, on birches, balsams, and firs. We come to a crossing. The train whistles and cars wait as we pass through a little town. We spot a Mobil station, and some grown-up remarks about how unusual it is to "see a Mobil station this close to the North Pole." My mother chuckles.

Ian wipes steam from the window and looks out. In a clearing is a farmhouse, candles in each window. A man wearing a Santa hat steps onto the front porch and waves to us. The train picks up speed, and we rush through forests of dusky pines, the outlines of hills in the distance. There are fewer houses on winding roads; the snow deepens. In the woods, faraway lights from faraway cottages flicker in the dark. Looking up at the sky (for reindeer?), Ian, struggling around the giant nougat candy in his cheek, says, "It's so nice, Mummy."

"There's a swing year," my mother whispers to me, "Usually around seven or eight years old. They want to believe in Santa still, but everything—their friends, maybe an older brother, their own reasoning—points to not believing. The eight-year-olds lobby hard for you to tell them about Santa's real identity. But you can see them wavering," she says. "They hedge their bets, because they think if they don't believe, they won't get any presents. So for a while, they decide to believe."

The train slows; we must be getting close. Doors open and conductors in crisp blue uniforms and hats stride through. The lights come up and the noise level, if possible, goes up. I prepare Ian for the North Pole: He'll need to wear his hat, scarf, and mittens.

"He knows if you've been bad or good?" he asks me.

"He does," I say. "But you have been very, very good. You were born that way."

Helped by elves in red velvet, we step off the train and walk through a tunnel of elves holding lanterns along a path up toward Santa's workshop. Outside the workshop, elves drag a huge red sack of toys toward Santa's parked sleigh.

"Mom, this is cooool," Ian whispers, very serious.

Inside, hundreds of children sit and kneel in rows before a big stage. There are backdrops—illustrations from The Polar Express. An old man dressed in a bathrobe sits on a chair on the stage and reads from the book— he is playing the part of the boy in the book, at the end of his life, remembering his visit to the North Pole. When he gets to the part where the boy receives a bell from Santa, a bell whose ring he still hears, because he still believes, all the little profiles strain to see. Where is Santa?

Elves scurry around, seeming to prepare. Some dads practice ho-ho-ho's. The sprinkling music of a dulcimer does little to dampen the gathering commotion that comes from Santa-waiting.

When it is almost too late, Santa comes in, "Ho Ho Ho," he bellows. He strides past us, seeming to greet every child. Ian hides his head in my lap, Santa looks over his sleigh, checks the fittings, confers with elves. The man in the bathrobe finishes the story. In the end, here at the North Pole, every child will receive a bell from Santa's sleigh to take home.

Elves help us back onto the train, and we chug back toward North Conway. It's warm inside. The lights dim, the train rocks and creaks. The singers in blue velvet walk down the aisle, slowly singing "Silent Night." It's past the bedtimes of all the children—and some of the adults. Within a few minutes, most are asleep.

I look down at my sleeping, rosy-cheeked son, who's probably content in the knowledge that Santa exists and that he somehow knows that Ian wants more than anything to get a glow-in-the-dark Hot Wheels car on Christmas morning. I hear bells softly jingling from within PolarFleece pockets and mittened fists—a couple here and there, then a whole chorus of them as we hit a rough patch on the tracks. I look over at my mother and I know she hears the bells too, and she just smiles.

When couples lived their entire lives in the same community, the reality of "home" for Christmas was more defined. The annual pilgrimage was anticipated keenly by children and grandchildren alike, and recollected as one of the most nurturing celebrations of family life. The anticipation is evoked breathlessly in the nineteenth-century poem on the following page, whose unidentified author describes a slow holiday journey through the English countryside.

Even today, with families scattered about the American map, the idea of home is precious, perhaps even more so given our transient ways. Memories of Christmases spent with our families glow brightly.

Our family traveled every other Christmas to my grandmother's farm in the northwest corner of Vermont. The large house, red barns,

OPPOSITE The title of this painting by D. H. Hilliker is simply *American Scene 1876*. It appeared on the cover of the February 1942 issue of *Railroad Magazine*. The details of traveling home for Christmas by train are present, right down to the expectant greeters on the platform.

BLIND MAN'S BLUFF
[Anonymous]

We shall have sport when Christmas comes,
When "snap-dragon" burns our fingers and thumbs:
We'll hang mistletoe over our dear little cousins,
And pull them beneath it and kiss them by dozens:
We shall have games at "Blind Man's Buff,"
And noise and laughter and romping enough.
We'll crown the plum-pudding with bunches of bay,
And roast all the chestnuts that come in our way;
And when Twelfth Night falls, we'll have such a cake
That as we stand round it the table shall quake.
We'll draw "King and Queen," and be happy together,
And dance old "Sir Roger" with hearts like a feather.
Home for the Holidays, here we go!
But this Fast train is really exceedingly slow!

and four hundred acres of rocky, tree-dotted pasture were located six miles north of St. Albans, a Central Vermont Railway station stop and a major CV maintenance facility. During the 1950s we made the trip by automobile, but one year, shortly after World War II, when highway travel was not the relatively carefree experience it is today, we took the train.

We lived in Rockland County, New York, on the west shore of the Hudson River, about twenty miles north of the George Washington Bridge. A neighbor drove us to the station in Haverstraw, where we caught a mid-afternoon local on the New York Central's West Shore division for Weehawken, New Jersey. There we boarded a ferry that took us across the Hudson to Manhattan. It was a cold, windy day, but my younger brother and I stood out on the deck and watched the city's towers loom higher as the boat approached them. A short cab ride delivered us to Pennsylvania Station. The journey had barely begun, and we had already been treated to a train ride, a boat trip, and a swift, bouncy traverse in a taxi.

Our train, the Montrealer, was not scheduled to depart until 8:25 PM. But we had arrived early, to make sure that our reservations and baggage checking were all in order, and to have dinner in the Savarin restaurant located in Penn Station. Dinner out was not a routine event in our family, and we looked forward to it eagerly. As we approached the restaurant we saw a man in a blue uniform mount the steps leading to the restaurant's entrance. He turned at the top of the steps, brandished a shiny bugle, and sounded a rousing fanfare. He then slowly descended the stairs and marched through the lofty main concourse, bugling loudly, to the departure gate for the Chicago-bound Broadway Limited, Pennsylvania Railroad train No. 29, the all-Pullman pride of the line. We learned that this

The graceful station at Haverstraw, New York, once a passenger stop on the New York Central's West Shore division, still stands, but is now occupied by a law firm. Rockland County artist Robert Burghardt titled his painting *Home for Christmas*. The train is moving north, looked after by a small boy and his dad, while a solitary traveler is greeted by a child and parent, and a couple share a holiday embrace.

ceremony was established in an effort to upstage the red-carpet rollout at Grand Central station that greeted passengers boarding the Twentieth Century Limited, the New York Central's westbound aristocrat.

The restaurant and the waiting room, two days before Christmas, were swarming with package- and baggage-laden travelers, some wearing anxious expressions, others looking weary, but most beaming with thoughts of festive reunions. After our holiday meal and a fidgety wait, we heard the departure announcement for the Montrealer. We trooped down the long staircase to track level, where a mob of passengers, porters, conductors, and sleeping-car attendants were busy sorting each other out.

We were directed to a car with ten sections and three double bedrooms. We peered into the bedrooms as we squeezed down the narrow hallway, and they looked cozy and luxurious, obviously intended for royalty, not for the likes of us. Our overnight accommodations were upper and lower berth sections, at present in their facing-seat configuration. My brother and I dug out a small stash of comic books from a bag retained from the family suitcase inventory now residing in the baggage car. Moments later a barely perceptible nudge declared the train's departure. I peered out the window as the train gathered speed, and watched the platform, just minutes ago teeming with people and now all but deserted, slip by.

I carried a Montrealer route guide, and noted that the train would soon cross the perilous-sounding Hell Gate Bridge on its way to Connecticut. From New York to Springfield, Massachusetts, the train would be conveyed by a New York, New Haven, and Hartford engine and crew. In Springfield, shortly after midnight, the Boston and Maine would take charge. I wondered if I could stay awake that long. Three hours after that, in White River Junction, Vermont, the Central Vermont Railway assumed control. St. Albans, our destination, was scheduled to be reached at 6:02 AM.

We rumbled across the Hell Gate Bridge without incident. In the distance, New York City sparkled brightly. The train stopped briefly in Stamford and Bridgeport, and when the conductor announced "Next stop—

OPPOSITE Holiday turmoil in Chicago's North Western Railroad station is rendered by Norman Rockwell for a 1944 *Saturday Evening Post* cover. Rockwell posed many of the subjects first in photographs, including the redhead in the center of the picture who complained to Rockwell that the posing didn't take long enough.

New Haven," Dad announced that it was time for bed. He led the way to the men's lounge and bathroom at the end of the car, and by the time we returned to our section it had been miraculously converted into upper and lower berths, complete with dark green curtains, and a narrow ladder ascending to the upper berth. My little brother insisted on the upper berth, but I didn't mind since this meant I could look out the window whenever I wanted to. My brother clambered happily up the ladder to the upper, and I cozied into the lower. I noted some mysterious netting with an elasticized top attached to the wall, a light switch, a tiny fan, and a narrow shelf. Dad explained that the netting was for our clothes, which we'd changed out of when we put on our pajamas and robes in the lounge.

A lower berth, of the type occupied by the author during his holiday journey home to Vermont. More than half a century later, the accommodation still looks inviting.

OPPOSITE Another Pullman advertisement, this one from the December 1948 issue of *National Geographic*, depicted three homeward-bound passages. The family group, along with the two solitary travelers, are all seen in the picture at the top of the ad.

I pleaded to keep the window shade up a while longer, and dad agreed, warning me not to stay awake too long past my accustomed bedtime. Fat chance. I stared out the window, mesmerized by clanging grade crossings, the flash of small-town stations, automobile headlights streaming past, the train whistle's hoot, and the cadenced clickety-clack of steel wheels crossing rail joints. As the Montrealer slowed for New Haven I could see the ghostly shapes of engines, and dozens of passenger and freight cars in the dim yard lights. Not long after that I was asleep.

It was still dark when I awoke. The train had stopped. The shade had been pulled down while I slept, but I was able to peer around the edge, and I saw the station sign for Essex Junction. This was the stop for Burlington, Vermont's biggest city, where we would visit my maternal grandparents for the New Year's weekend. I knew we were now only a half-hour or so from St. Albans, or would be if the train would only start moving. I gathered up my clothes, parted the curtain, and stepped into the aisle. Mom and Dad were up, and Dad told me that the train would be delayed at the

Christmas Cargo

1. They'll be home for Christmas! There are miles of snow and mountains ahead. But this family will spend *their* night before Christmas snug and secure in their Pullman compartment. They bring gifts for her folks back home. But the greatest gift to that proud Grandfather and Grandmother will be the sight of their first grandchild.

2. He'll be home for Christmas! He's a hard working trouble-shooter for his company, and business *almost* kept him away for Christmas. But there'll be no disappointments in this father's house tomorrow morning. Traveling Pullman, he and his presents will arrive safe and sound right in the heart of town, just a stone's throw from Christmas at home.

3. She'll be home for Christmas! "Dear Mother and Dad," she wrote. "I'll be home for Christmas with a straight 'A' for the quarter. Don't you think that deserves going Pullman?" It does and it did. But more important, her mother and father will sleep as soundly tonight as she will, knowing she's traveling the safest, most comfortable way to be home for Christmas.

To be sure *you'll* be home for Christmas

Go Pullman

**THE <u>SAFEST</u>, MOST <u>COMFORTABLE</u> WAY
TO <u>GET</u> <u>THERE</u>!**

© 1948, THE PULLMAN COMPANY

station for a few minutes while something called a hotbox was serviced. I dressed quickly, willing the train into motion.

After a length of time that seemed, to a ten-year-old, interminable, the train began to move again. It was now running almost an hour late, and the snowy landscape was beginning to brighten. Our berths had disappeared, and my brother and I sat opposite each other, counting the minutes and the miles, waiting tensely for the conductor to call out St. Albans. At last the announcement sounded through the car, and the train began to slow;

soon it crept into the huge covered train shed and stopped. Grandmother was waiting, and somehow we wedged ourselves and all our luggage and gift bags into her Buick. My brother and I sat on the front seat, shivering with the cold and Christmas ecstasy.

Compare our modest accommodations with those taken for granted by the Vanderbilt clan as they gathered for a Christmas family reunion more than a half-century before ours. In his book *The Vanderbilt Legend*, Wayne Andrews wrote; "On Christmas Eve, 1895, the personal Wagner palace cars of many members of the House of Vanderbilt rolled into sidings near Asheville, North Carolina. Dr. and Mrs. Seward Webb, their children and domestics; Mr. William Kissam Vanderbilt I, and his domestics; Mr. and Mrs. Cornelius Vanderbilt II, their children and domestics, then alighted and entered carriages that conveyed them to Biltmore, the domain of George Washington Vanderbilt II." The private cars were spotted on sidings placed for the Vanderbilts' convenience by the Southern Railroad Company. No Buicks for them, even if they had been invented.

Residing somewhere between my family's economy-minded travel arrangements and the Vanderbilt entitlements, trains such as the Broadway Limited, the thoroughbred heralded by bugle calls, earned the affections of thousands of travelers, even those forced by unyielding circumstances to travel on Christmas Eve. The article on page 113, from the December 1947 issue of *Trains*, describes a Christmas Eve aboard the Pennsy's premier flyer.

Twenty years later, the Broadway had lost its all-Pullman panache, having been merged with the General. Other lines, including the New York Central and the Santa Fe, had also downgraded passenger service, and in many cases eliminated it. It was still possible in the late 1960s to travel in a semblance of style on the remaining name trains, but the long-term prospects for passenger travel were dimming daily.

One of the B&O's celebrated passenger trains, the National Limited, was still running between St. Louis and Washington, D.C. in 1967, albeit with coaches only. Bill Snorteland, a junior at Ohio University in Athens,

OPPOSITE The soaring train shed attached to the Vermont Central station and offices at St. Albans, Vermont, was built in 1866 of red Vermont brick, and nearly survived to its one-hundredth birthday. There were four arched openings at either end, and the shed measured 351 feet long and 84 feet wide. In this picture by Jim Shaughnessy, a light holiday snow is drifting down on a steam engine in the south portal as well as a setout sleeping car from Boston.

The Wise Men

Of the Twentieth Century travel over the Lake Shore & Michigan Southern Ry.
The old gentleman in the picture is joyfully telling his friends how, detained
until the last moment by business and sorely disappointed at the prospect of a
Christmas away from home, he happened to learn of the fast service of the
"20th CENTURY LIMITED," how he caught the train just in time, and thus
after all is assured of a merry Christmas with his folks.
For information about travel over the Lake Shore address A. J. SMITH,
G. P. & T. A., Cleveland, Ohio.
To travelers everywhere the Lake Shore wishes a Merry Christmas.

"Look out
for the
20th Century Limited"

America's premier train is the "20th Century Limited;" the train that, in practically a
single night, traverses the one thousand miles of distance between Chicago and New York, leaving
after the business day is done and arriving *before* the business day begins.
Even the boy in the picture has caught the spirit which the splendid service of the
Lake Shore—New York Central
route arouses among its patrons and which the "20th Century Limited" so truly exemplifies.
The Lake Shore is the most comfortable fast service route in America, and the "20th
Century Limited" is the foremost example of American passenger train service.
Chicago—New York—18 Hours.
For copy of "Book of Trains" and information about your travel matters, address undersigned,
C. F. DALY,   A. J. SMITH,
Passenger Traffic Manager, Chicago, Ill.   General Passenger Agent, Cleveland, O.

These two ads, placed by the
Lake Shore & Michigan Southern
Railway, later part of the New
York Central System, promote
the Twentieth Century Limited.
Both ran in a magazine named
Current Literature. The Wise Men
appeared in 1903, just a year
after the Century's maiden voyage, and the returning-father
scene ran two years later.

PAGE 115: This is the advertisement described in the accom-
panying piece "Christmas Eve
on the Broadway." The child has
had the good sense to leave
her roomette door open to facil-
itate Santa's delivery.

planned to travel part of his way home to New York on the National, but
a friend traveling north asked him if he'd like a ride, and Snorteland joined
him as far as Columbus. There he could catch a Pennsylvania Railroad train
straight through to New York, avoiding a change of trains in Washington.

The Columbus Union Station was a holiday madhouse when Snorteland got there. The Penn Texas was due out at 7:00 PM, but the throngs
crowding to the train's gate encouraged him to wait for the 9:00 PM departure of the Spirit of St. Louis. Another mob descended on that train,
but this time Snorteland was closer to the front of the line. He got aboard
and found a lumpy seat in an ancient day coach, which had been added to
the Spirit's consist to accommodate the holiday hordes. He sat as far as
Pittsburgh with a soldier on leave from Fort Leonard Wood, who left

Christmas Eve of every year finds some thousand souls aboard the country's overnight limiteds while old Saint Nick and his arctic steeds whirl mystically through the night sky overhead. And while family groups and friends everywhere congregate in homes aglow with the festive Christmas spirit, the Christmas Eve travelers, luggage in hand, trudge along station platforms and swing aboard the trains that will be home to them for the most important, most looked-forward-to night of the year.

Last December 24, Chicago's Union Station thronged with thousands of late-afternoon travelers, most of whom were bound for towns and cities only a few hours' journey away. Traffic had been so heavy all afternoon that yard movements had been hampered, and only a few trains were being spotted on station tracks in time for scheduled loading and departure. A large crowd had gathered at the entrance gate of the Minneapolis-bound Afternoon Zephyrs, whose Vista Dome cars were visible through the gates.

CHRISTMAS EVE
ON THE
BROADWAY

✴

Al Rung

The minute hand of the station clock moved resolutely onward, and it was 4:10 before the Pennsylvania's 4:15 Detroit Arrow opened for loading. At the far left gate the GM&O's Abraham Lincoln to St. Louis was loading, well in advance of her scheduled 4:50 departure, while at gate 22 a small group of passengers waited quietly for the train announcement to be placed on the board.

At 4:25 the lights on the gate board were switched on and the red-and-gold train announcement was lifted into position: "4:30 PM, the Broadway Limited, 16-hour train—Philadelphia, Newark, New York," the heading read. Below this was listed the consist of the train.

The passengers filed through the gate, calling out their space reservations to the gateman: "Roomette 2, car 285," "Bedroom E, car 289." The train was hamdsome in its highly polished coat of red and gold, and the red, white, and blue Broadway Limited tail sign was a brilliant contrast to the darkened train shed.

At 4:41 the Broadway began to move slowly out of the station, past the Abraham Lincoln, whose modern coaches had been filled to the very last seat. Two New York Central coaches had thoughtfully been added to that train in anticipation of the heavy travel. The twin-unit diesel that topped off the "Abe's" consist stabbed its headlight in through the rounded rear windows of the Broadway's streamlined Skyline View observation car as a departing gesture.

Gathering speed as it passed the Twelfth Street coach yards, the Broadway passed the Burlington's Denver Zephyr backing into the station for its nightly sprint to the Rockies.

Several passengers boarded at Englewood, and then the Broadway began to dig in for its race over the Pennsy's speedway from Englewood to Fort Wayne—a stretch of track dear to every Pennsylvania man.

About five persons sat in the observation lounge, and all were sipping drinks served by the lounge attendant. The ten-year-old son of a New York couple was bombarding his very tolerant father with a barrage of questions and comments in a tone of voice that clearly indicated that the youngster was "playing to the galleries." Finally his mother explained that he was "tired," and led him away to their drawing room. This course of action was visibly appreciated by the rest of the passengers.

The steel mills of Gary flashed by, then glimpses of towns and of cars halted at grade crossings while the Broadway hurtled past on its lightning-fast dash to Fort Wayne.

Some six cars ahead, the dining car was the center of attraction. A courtly steward assigned the diners to their tables in the attractively decorated car. All tables were soon filled. Tablecloths on the Broadway dining cars differ from other cloths used on the Pennsylvania system; they are a rich copper-brown shade. The menu this Christmas Eve was palate-tickling: the pièce de résistance was braised ribs of beef, preceded by cream-of-pea soup and PRR assorted salad. Stewed onions and stringless beans were the vegetable offerings, topped off by a number of desserts, most interesting of which was probably the hot deep-dish apple pie. The meal would have made the most exacting gourmet weep tears of joy, and the service provided by the hand-picked crew left nothing to be desired.

Back in the lounge car a beautiful young actress and her husband played a few quiet rounds of cards. A middle-aged manufacturer was—between sips of beer—engrossed in a pocket-size mystery thriller, while a young chemical engineer read the December issue of Trains (provided in the lounge cars of crack Pennsylvania trains). He finally paused at the Pennsylvania Railroad advertisement entitled "'Twas the Night before Christmas." It pictured a PRR trainman, in company with Santa himself, smiling down on a sleeping youngster as she slept in her roomette.

"Step into cars aglow with good cheer and good fellowship," said the ad. The chemist showed it to the smiling lounge attendant and said, "I think it would be a splendid act of good fellowship on the part of the Pennsylvania Railroad if it were to serve a free round of drinks tonight." The porter, who had listened with amused anticipation, broke into a hearty guffaw that soon had the other occupants of the car laughing.

"That laugh is worth a million words," said the manufacturer.

The chemist grinned. "Well, if Santa isn't going to visit us tonight I'm going to turn in," he said, and after exchanging a "Merry Christmas" with the other passengers he left the car.

A beauty-parlor owner had been staring idly about the car. He expressed interest in the Broadway's master bedrooms, and as both were vacant that night the porter showed him one of the luxurious rooms with its shower bath, at that time the only such accommodation in the country except for a similar car on the Broadway's twin running mate, the Chicago-Washington Liberty Limited.

Christmas Eve in 1947 was cold and clear, and bright moonlight bathed the rolling fields of Indiana and Ohio as the Broadway streaked eastward. From the cushioned quiet of a darkened room you could plainly see the brilliantly lighted farmhouses and town residences, and sense the pre-Christmas activity going on inside. Glimpses of colorful Christmas trees could be seen through parlor windows, and in many windows electric candles were glowing.

The gleaming Tuscan-red limited drifted to a halt at Crestline, Ohio, and with ghostly quiet the shadowy figures of station workers appeared and began to check the train's mechanical equipment and fill the water reservoirs of the Pullmans. Then the station lights of Crestline glided gently backward as the Broadway slipped away into the night.

At Toledo Junction a steam-shrouded M-1 (4-8-2) freight engine waited in the darkness for the Broadway to clear the main line and enable the Toledo-Pittsburgh nightly merchandiser to again get under way toward the Steel City.

Mansfield and Orrville flashed by, and on the station

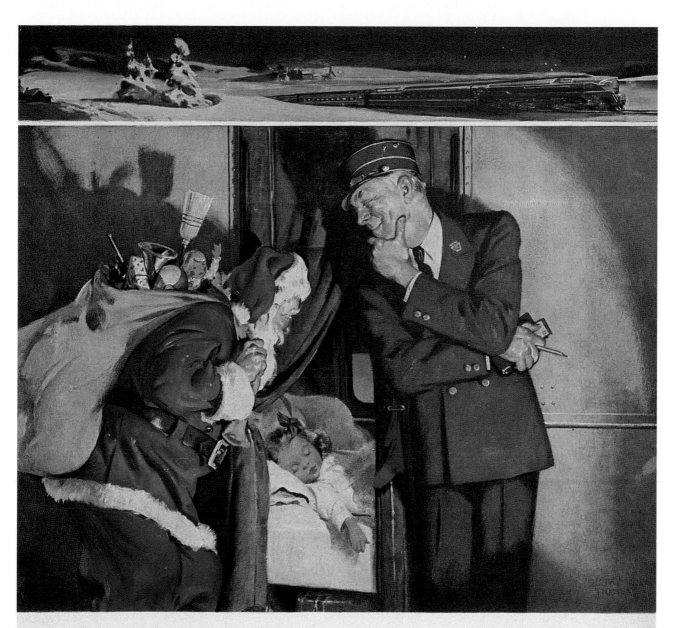

'twas the night before Christmas...

...And this little miss asleep in a cozy roomette, her stocking hung high in great expectation, symbolizes the spirit you find aboard Pennsylvania Railroad's great East-West Fleet at this season of the year. Step into cars aglow with good cheer and good fellowship ... glance at the array of beribboned gifts heaped high in racks and rooms.

Stroll into the Dining Car and enjoy the festive foods of the day ... get a good night's sleep in a comfortable bed—arrive refreshed. And above all, enjoy the peace of mind that comes from knowing your train will get you there—conveniently, and at low cost. All aboard ... to a Merry Christmas and Happy New Year!

PENNSYLVANIA RAILROAD

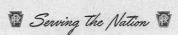

Serving the Nation

platforms stood truckloads of parcel post that wouldn't arrive in time for Christmas—mute testimony to the over-loading of postal and express facilities during the un-precedented 1947 holiday rush.

It was getting late now, and most homes were in dark-ness, although—considering the hour—a surprising num-ber were ablaze with light. You could imagine children's Christmas gifts being placed under the family tree, trimmed with patience and loving care though possibly at the expense of a strained disposition or two.

The Broadway raced for the Ohio River with the spring-ing steely stride of a giant greyhound. Up ahead you could see the speeding three-unit Electro-Motive diesel as it swung gracefully around the curves and under sig-nal bridges whose yellow position-light signals jumped from a vertical to a horizontal position as the diesel thun-dered past below.

Then down the mighty Ohio, both of whose banks are lined with the heavy industry that is an outpost of the Pittsburgh area activity. On the adjacent track, fore-runners of the westbound night fleet flashed by with a roar and a colorful blaze of light. Then all was still throughout the cold moonlit valley.

After a brief stop at Pittsburgh the train swung past East Liberty and Greensburg, then twisted through the rugged valley and over the bridge at Johnstown, and curved away into the night as steel furnaces lit the sky.

The Broadway was running right on the minute before it crawled to a halt at the summit of the Alleghenies, only a few miles from the famed Horseshoe Curve. Then the stillness became apparent. Nothing stirred that night on the famous four-track main line that climbed the dark, hushed mountains. Inside the insulated, streamlined Pullmans, light shone softly on carpeted aisles, but as in the famous Christmas Eve poem, "not a creature was stir-ring"—and there are no mice on the Broadway.

The forward lounge car, flooded only a few hours before with the cheerfulness of bright light, smart decor, and gay passengers, was now the peacefully dark head-quarters of the train crew. Only one trainman remained in the car, his bulk silhouetted against a window.

"Forty-eight's got engine trouble," he said.

Soon the trainmen returned, their electric lanterns jab-bing beams of light around the wood-paneled walls of the lounge car. "We're going to back to MG Tower and run around 48," said the conductor.

Before the Broadway began to backup, the Detroit-Washington Red Arrow, train No. 68, stepped smartly past on the adjacent track with her K-4s sprightly exhaust chuckling proudly as it bypassed the streamlined, diesel-powered, blue-ribbon train. And so the K-4 will be remembered—valiantly turning in a last great perform-ance before being retired from main-line service to be replaced by more modern power.

After backing to the tower the Broadway switched to another track and started slowly down the mountain. The General (No. 48) had remedied the trouble in her diesel by this time, however, and so preceded the Broadway around graceful, moonlit Horseshoe Curve and into Altoona, heart of the Pennsylvania system.

The drab station and sooty Civil War-era train shed at Altoona deceptively camouflage the fact that here is the home of the great spirit that nightly directs and drives the Pennsy's great east-west fleet over the rails—the spirit that is present in every operating department, shop, and office the length and breadth of the far-flung Pennsylvania network. The executive formality and ele-gance, the polished desks, and occasional touches of glit-ter that are a part of operations in the large eastern cities won't be found in Altoona. You will have to look hard to detect even the slightest outward indication of this timeless spirit. But look closely at the small group of trainmen standing on the station platform—the men who loudly profess disdain for any sentiment about railroads—as they brace themselves against the biting wind of the cold winter night to watch the Broadway slip away to the east. The Broadway is more than just "No. 28" to these men.

For the next two hours and twenty minutes the Broadway raced over the Middle Division, through the historic Juniata Valley that once was laced with Indian foot trails, later to give way to plodding Conestoga wagons and canal boats. Dark, towering mountains looked down on the speeding train.

In the gray half-light of dawn at Harrisburg, the diesel units were cut off and a green and gold GG-1 electric engine was substituted for the last high-speed dash over the tensely scheduled Philadelphia and New York divisions. Then the Broadway raced along the broad Susquehanna River, lined with huge plants of the Bethlehem Steel Company. Past the slumbering army air base at Middletown she went, then over the rolling hills of beautiful Lancaster County. She left the deserted Lancaster station behind in a swirling eighty-miles-an-hour rush, crossed the high stone bridge at Coatesville, and headed for the Main Line section of Philadelphia.

Coasting through Paoli, western end of the famous Main Line, the Broadway entered the fashionable residential section that stretches for some twenty miles along the Pennsylvania's rails to the city limits of Philadelphia. The early morning sun that shone down on the Main Line that Christmas morning reflected from the vine-covered embankment and from the foliage of residential lawns, a warm blending of greens and browns that brightened the cold of the day.

Dining-car attendance for the Christmas breakfast was light; Philadelphia passengers apparently had arranged to have breakfast with their families on arrival—and the majority of Broadway passengers were destined for Philadelphia. It was about 9:05 AM when the stream-lined GG-1 brought the crack blue-ribbon flyer to a halt at North Philadelphia Station. The eastbound platform was unusually quiet for this hour of the morning—it is usually jammed with passengers bound for New York—and the ceremony of unloading luggage onto the platform and tipping the porters was quickly accomplished.

In a matter of seconds the Broadway was rolling noiselessly along the platform, bearing passengers, trainmen, and porters home to New York for Christmas morning get-togethers with their families. And as the streamlined observation car receded down the straight steelway that is the Pennsylvania's main line to New York, Philadelphia passengers walked downstairs to the taxi stands to board cabs that took them to all parts of the city, each to participate, a few minutes later, in the happy festivities that have made Christmas morning a joyous occasion throughout the civilized world.

behind a copy of the *Playboy Joke Book*, explaining that he didn't dare take it home. At Altoona his train was sidetracked to allow the eastbound Broadway Limited to pass, which it did moments later, churning through a swirling snow squall.

Due to the snow and the oversubscribed passenger lists, the Spirit of St. Louis arrived at New York's Pennsylvania Station about an hour late. But a glance at a newspaper headline told Snorteland that he should count his blessings. A bridge over the Ohio River, less than fifty miles from his campus, had collapsed under a heavy load of holiday traffic, and many lives had been lost. Snorteland had occasionally crossed that bridge. He said a prayer of thanks for the safe passage afforded by the Pennsylvania Railroad and the Spirit of St. Louis.

Another memoir recounted by a collegiate traveler appears on the facing page, given voice by Nick Carraway, the narrator of F. Scott Fitzgerald's *The Great Gatsby*. These are Fitzgerald's homeward-yearning memories, of course, touching on one of the novel's principal themes, and timeless in the evocation.

Still another undergraduate headed for his home in the Midwest, Robert Ralston, began his trip at Chicago's Union Station on Christmas Eve in 1969, but only as a last resort. His plane ticket to Omaha was useless, thanks to a paralyzing blizzard howling across Nebraska. He took a local train from his campus in a northern suburb of Chicago, bound for Union Station, where he would catch the Union Pacific's City of Los Angeles. That noble limited, only fifteen months removed from Amtrak anonymity, would carry him to Columbus, Nebraska, fifteen miles from his home in Schuyler.

The City left on time, and enjoyed smooth running for several hours before entering the storm zone in western Iowa. A twenty-five minute stop

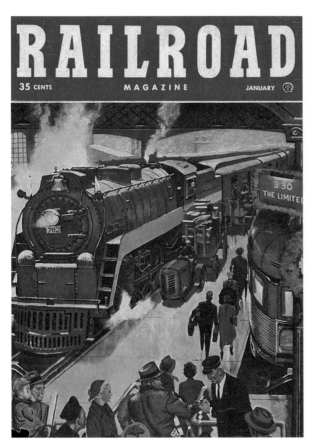

A busy scene of Christmas travelers portrays them showing their tickets to the conductor, while mountains of luggage and packages wait to be put aboard. This picture is also titled *Home for Christmas* (with Wabash in parentheses following the title), perhaps designating artist Herb Mott's favorite railroad. The cover appeared in 1952.

was scheduled in Omaha, during which Ralston called home to make sure someone was planning to pick him up in Columbus, now just an hour and a half distant. He was told that nothing was moving on the roads in and around his hometown, that eighteen inches of snow had already fallen, and another six to ten inches were expected.

The idea of being snowbound in Columbus, fifteen miles from home, was intolerable. Ralston thought about his family huddled cozily at home in Schuyler. He thought about the tiny station there, just six blocks away from the house. He knew that the City of Los Angeles did not stop in Schuyler, and that a local train hadn't served the town in more than three years. Still, it was Christmas Eve, he was tantalizingly close to home, and he had absolutely nothing to lose by asking. He mustered up his courage and what he hoped was an effective mix of charm and desperation, and explained his plight to the conductor. Expecting a curt and deflating "no," he was amazed to hear the frowning gentleman say, "Oh, what the heck,

F. SCOTT FITZGERALD
From The Great Gatsby

★

One of my most vivid memories is of coming back West from prep school and later from college at Christmas time. Those who went farther than Chicago would gather in the old dim Union Station at six o'clock of a December evening, with a few Chicago friends, already caught up into their own holiday gayeties, to bid them a hasty good-by. I remember the fur coats of the girls returning from Miss This-or-That's and the chatter of frozen breath and the hands waving overhead as we caught sight of old acquaintances, and the matchings of invitations: "Are you going to the Ordways'? the Herseys'? the Schultzes'?" and the long green tickets clasped tight in our gloved hands. And last the murky yellow cars of the Chicago, Milwaukee & St. Paul railroad looking cheerful as Christmas itself on the tracks beside the gate.

When we pulled out into the winter night and the real snow, our snow, began to stretch out beside us and twinkle against the windows, and the dim lights of small Wisconsin stations moved by, a sharp wild brace came suddenly into the air. We drew in deep breaths of it as we walked back from dinner through the cold vestibules, unutterably aware of our identity with this country for one strange hour, before we melted indistinguishably into it again.

That's my Middle West—not the wheat or the prairies or the lost Swede towns, but the thrilling returning trains of my youth, and the street lamps and sleigh bells in the frosty dark and the shadows of holly wreaths thrown by lighted windows on the snow.

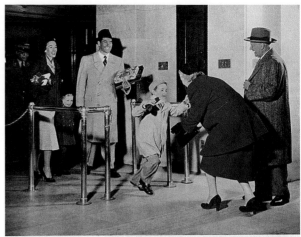

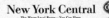

Little Girl, Big Date!
And she'll keep it, <u>weather</u> or <u>no</u>, on New York Central

A date with Santa . . . at Grandmother's, far away? That's just *too* important to risk being delayed on winter highways or skyways. Better go Central for sure!

Or maybe you *are* "Santa Claus" . . . heading home after a pre-Christmas business trip. Well, sir, relax! Order a famous New York Central dinner. Join the holiday good cheer in the lounge. Get

a good, sound Water Level Route sleep. You'll be home as planned. Rested and ready to put on your red suit and white beard. Ready to enjoy every minute of Christmas day!

* * *

Yes, whatever *your* holiday trip . . . let New York Central give it all-weather comfort and all-weather certainty *no other travel can match!*

People are the Nicest Presents! Send a ticket home to someone you want with you at Christmas time. Ask your New York Central ticket agent how to send prepaid coach or Pullman tickets as gifts.

New York Central
The Water Level Route—You Can Sleep

Many Happy Returns!
Let New York Central <u>weatherproof</u> your holiday home-coming!

Home for Christmas. Magic words! But where's the magic to keep stormbound skyways and highways from turning the promise into bitter disappointment?

You'll find just such magic on New York Central's great all-weather fleet. You'll ride in

a cozily air-conditioned climate, with plenty of room to roam. You'll enjoy tempting, freshly prepared meals. You'll sleep, really sleep, on the smooth Water Level Route.

And, above all, you'll give your holiday plans a *certainty* no other travel can match!

HOLIDAY ALL THE WAY! Join the good fellowship in the club car. Relax in your lean-back coach seat . . . or in the privacy of your Pullman hotel-room-on-wheels. Arrive refreshed and ready for the fun of an old-fashioned family Christmas.

New York Central
The Water Level Route—You Can Sleep

A New York Central ad from 1950. At that time, air and highway transportation were beginning to alter significantly how people traveled, but those modes were susceptible to adverse weather conditions, especially during winters in the northeast and Midwest—hence the emphasis on "weather or no."

This ad, from the December 10, 1951, issue of *Time* magazine is a follow-up to the ad on the left. The little girl's mom and dad are shown, as well as her brother, who is running into the welcoming embrace of his grandmother. Never mind that these are all models. One of our favorite Christmas maxims applies here: "It's the thought that counts."

we're on time, it's Christmas Eve, and you're really stuck." Ralston was instructed to be in the vestibule of a designated car when the train passed through Rogers, a town eight miles east of Schuyler. If he wasn't there, the conductor warned, there would be no stop in Schuyler.

Ralston was in place with time to spare. The City of Los Angeles ground to a slow stop in front of the Schuyler depot, and the conductor beamed his flashlight on a two-foot-high snowdrift, into which Ralston was to alight. He did so, somehow maintaining his balance as well as his grip on a large suitcase and two shopping bags laden with gifts. He hailed the conductor with a hearty "thank you" and "merry Christmas," and watched the train begin to roll into the snowy night.

He stood across the tracks from the station, and when the long train had finally moved past he saw the glow from a flashlight held by the freight agent who was understandably curious as to why the City of Los Angeles, usually nothing more than a hurtling blur, had stopped. Curiosity turned to incredulity when Ralston explained that the train had stopped to let him off. Several minutes later, his family was no less thunderstruck when their snow-mantled son banged on the front door, after a slog through the knee-high snowfall. It became a family legend: the last paying customer to depart a Union Pacific train in Schuyler, Nebraska.

Almost everyone dreams of a white Christmas, except those forced to deal with its inconveniences. In December 1945, Fred Houser was on his way to

The Denver Zephyr, speeding through a Christmas snowstorm in 1937. On November 11, 1934, the Burlington placed the Pioneer Zephyr, a train similar to this one, into service between Lincoln, Nebraska, and Kansas City. It was the nation's first diesel-powered streamlined train.

Greenville, Pennsylvania, part of a massive deployment attempting to return tens of thousands of service troops to their homes in time for Christmas.

The weather was hospitable in Lamy, New Mexico, where Houser joined a standing-room-only muster on the Santa Fe's California Limited,

You ARE THEIR MOST PRECIOUS GIFT!

GO HOME FOR CHRISTMAS . . .
you and your family are the one present the folks at home will appreciate above all others

Think of the joy on their faces when they meet you at the station! Think of the happiness in their hearts over having you back for the holidays! And imagine the fun you'll all have . . . being together once more for a real old-fashioned Christmas!

Any weather is good weather in a Pullman. Pack your bags . . . make your reservations . . . and get going! You'll be traveling in the greatest comfort, dependability and safety known to modern transportation.

And — almost before you know it — you'll be there. You'll arrive completely rested and relaxed . . . bringing the one precious gift that is beyond all price . . . "Yourself"!

Why not call your travel or ticket agent now? He'll be glad to give you details on today's low Pullman prices. You'll be surprised at the modest cost of taking the family home the comfortably fast and dependable way . . . by Pullman. The Pullman Company, Chicago.

Copyright 1938, The Pullman Company

New Bedroom Suite Now Lower Priced. This suite for 2, 3 or 4 people is ideal for families, students on vacation and other travel groups. It consists of two connecting private rooms, each with a lower and upper bed, complete toilet facilities, separately controlled ventilation, heating and cooling. Where the new-type bedrooms are available, these may be converted—by folding or sliding back the intermediate partition—into a spacious suite for dining, card playing and other group activities. The cost is the same for 2, 3 or 4 people —and is no more than the price of a drawing room.*

(Plus, of course, first class rail fare for each passenger.)

Go RAIL AND *Pullman*   THE COMFORTABLE AND SURE WAY TO GET THERE . . . WITH ALL THE SPEED TRAINS SAFE!

The Pullman Company weighed in with holiday advertising of its own during the late 1930s, hoping to tempt overnight travelers in search of greater comforts than those available in a chair coach.

OPPOSITE Santa is pictured opening his sack to unveil the fleet of New York Central stream-liners serving Eastern and Mid-western cities in 1949. These were just the pedigreed transports; many less-heralded Central trains also brought travelers home.

but by the time the train reached the plains of eastern Colorado it was enveloped by a blizzard and running six hours behind schedule. The storm followed the train eastward, and in Topeka a grade-crossing mishap added another delay. The train made it to Kansas City almost twelve hours late, where it sat for another two hours. Houser did manage to find a place to sit in Kansas City, thanks to several departures there. His seat was next to the vestibule in a barely serviceable day coach, and every time the door was opened he was stung with a gust of blowing snow. Some holiday cheer was provided by a group of stalwart residents of Chillicothe, Illinois, who stood in a freezing gale and a foot of snow and served hot coffee and doughnuts to the troops.

The California Limited limped into Chicago's Dearborn Station more than thirteen hours delayed. This added another night to Houser's journey, spent aboard the Erie Railroad's Atlantic Express. The tenacious storm accompanied him through Indiana, Ohio, and western Pennsylvania, and greeted his arrival in Greenville. Houser couldn't have cared less about the weather. His family was waiting on the station platform. He had made it home for Christmas.

Houser coped bravely with the discomforts that beset his journey. In the excerpt on page 124 from Lloyd C. Douglas's novel *Home for Christmas*, two sisters are traveling to a family reunion, reflecting haughtily on accommodations that Houser might have found luxurious.

Years from now, with any luck, folks will still be traveling home for Christmas, but it's less certain that they'll be able to do so by train. Every

LLOYD C. DOUGLAS
From Home for Christmas

✦

Nan Clayton, attractive in a brown fur-trimmed ensemble that accented the tawniness of her hair, and attended by a tall young fellow with a big C on his sweater, was waiting on the station platform when the snow-covered local—spouting billows of pungent steam from every valve and coupling—lumbered to a stop at the little Wimple station.

An impish smile puckered her lips as she watched an obliging trainman descend the steps with both arms and hands full of swagger baggage. She glanced up at her youthful companion and gave him a slow wink. Everything, she reflected happily, was proceeding as she had hoped.

"Claire, my dear," Gertrude had confided, after the red-cap in Detroit—apologetic because there was no parlor car—had disposed the baggage in the racks above their heads, "I have a feeling that Nan purposely recommended this awful train."

"I rather like it," Claire had replied. "I haven't been in a day coach since I don't know when. Takes me back to the days when a train ride was high adventure. There's something about the smell of it—coal cinders, red plush, varnish, all scrambled together—that erases half a lifetime."

Gertrude regarded her with a sardonic grin and observed that this poky train would probably erase the other half before they arrived. Eventually, however, the trainman was shouting "Wimple!"—exactly as in the old days, with such heavy stress on the first syllable that a bored traveler, unacquainted with the country, might be thought to say to himself, "Odd name for a town—Wimp!"

They came down the slippery steps gingerly and found themselves warmly embraced by their sister.

ELIZABETH BOWEN
From Home for Christmas

✦

This is meeting time again. Home is the magnet. The winter land roars and hums with the eager speed of return journeys. The dark is noisy and bright with late-night arrivals—doors thrown open, running shadows on snow, open arms, kisses, voices and laughter, laughter at everything and nothing. Inarticulate, giddying and confused are those original minutes of being back again. The very familiarity of everything acts like shock. Contentment has to be drawn in slowly, steadyingly, in deep breaths—there is so much of it. We rely on home not to change, and it does not, wherefore we give thanks. Again Christmas: abiding point of return. Set apart by its mystery, mood and magic, the season seems in a way to stand outside time. All that is dear, that is lasting, renews its hold on us: we are home again. . . .

The marquee on the Bijou Theater advertises *It's a Wonderful Life*, which places this holiday scene in 1946. The station sign reads Bedford Falls, the imaginary town in which Frank Capra's classic film takes place.

year Amtrak is forced to fight for a reasonable budget, while our government doles out inflated subsidies to the airlines, fails to penalize gas guzzlers, and continues to build highways. There was a time, not so long ago, when such plagues were undreamed of. Taking the train home for Christmas was a joyful routine. In her book *Home for Christmas*, published in 1957, Elizabeth Bowen portrayed the glow of holiday reunions. It is not difficult to imagine that the "roars and hums," and "eager speed" describe the progress of passenger trains charging across the land, filled with homeward-bound celebrants.

SOURCES

books

ANDREWS, WAYNE. *The Vanderbilt Legend*. New York: Harcourt Brace and Co., 1941.

BEEBE, LUCIUS. *Mansions on Rails*. Berkeley: Howell-North Books, 1959.

BEEBE, LUCIUS AND CLEGG, CHARLES. *The Trains We Rode*. Vol. 2. Berkeley: Howell-North Books, 1966.

BELLE, JOHN AND LEIGHTON, MAXINNE. *Grand Central: Gateway to a Million Lives*. New York: W. W. Norton & Company, 2000.

BOWEN, ELIZABETH. *Home For Christmas*. Englewood Cliffs, N.J.: Prentice Hall, Inc., 1957.

BRADLEY, BILL. *The Last Of The Great Stations: 40 Years of the Los Angeles Union Passenger Terminal*. Glendale, C.A.: Interurbans Publications, 1979.

BROWN, WALTER ROLLO. *I Travel By Train*.New York: D. Appleton-Century Co., 1939.

COHEN, RONALD D. AND McSHANE, STEPHEN G., eds. *Moonlight In Duneland*. Bloomington and Indianapolis: Indiana University Press, 1998.

COOK, RICHARD J. *The Twentieth Century Limited: 1938–1967*. Lynchburg, V.A.: TLC Publishing Inc., 1993.

DUBIN, ARTHUR D. *Some Classic Trains*. Waukesha, W.I.: Kalmbach Publishing Co., 1964.

HOLLANDER, RON. *All Aboard: The Story of Joshua Lionel Cowen and His Lionel Train Company*. New York: Workman Publishing Co., 1981.

MARSHALL, DAVID. *Grand Central*. New York: McGraw-Hill, Inc., 1946.

McCOMAS, TOM AND TUOHY, JAMES. *Lionel: A Collector's Guide and History, Volume VI*. Radnor, P.A.: Chilton Book Co., 1981.

OGBURN, CHARLTON. *Railroads: The Great American Adventure*. Washington, D.C.: The National Geographic Society, 1977.

PERATA, DAVID. *Those Pullman Blues: An Oral History of the African-American Railroad Attendant*. New York: Twayne Publishers, 1996.

PONZAL, DAN AND MILNE, BILL. *Lionel: A Century of Timeless Toy Trains*. Metro Books/Ziccardi, 2002.

ROSENBAUM, JOEL AND GALLO, TOM. *The Broadway Limited*. 2nd ed. Piscataway N.J.: Railpace Co., 2001.

STONE, DESMOND. *Alec Wilder In Spite Of Himself*. New York: Oxford University Press, 1999.

SCHAFER, MIKE AND WELSH, JOE. *Classic American Streamliners*. Osceola, W.I.: Motorbooks International Publishers and Wholesalers, 1997.

SOUTER, JERRY AND SOUTER, JANET. *American Flyer: Classic Toy Trains*. The Michael Friedman Publishing Group, 2002.

STOVER, JOHN F. *The Routledge Historical Atlas Of The American Railroads*. New York: Routledge, 1999.

WATSON, BRUCE. *The Man Who Changed How Boys And Toys Were Made*. New York: Penguin Group, 2002.

WHITAKER, ROGERS E.M. AND HISS, TONY. *All Aboard With E.M. Frimbo*. New York: Kodansha America Inc., 1996.

YENNE, BILL. *All Aboard: The Golden Age of American Rail Travel*. Greenwich, CT: Brompton Books, 1989.

articles

ANDERSON, BARRY. "Christmas on the High Iron." *Trains* (December 1999).

BENCHLEY, ROBERT. "A Good Old Fashioned Christmas." *Harper & Row* (1927, renewed by Gertrude Benchley, 1955).

BETTS, MARGARET. "Grandfather's Allergy." *Trains* (December 1996).

BUNTE, JIM. "Where Every Kid Wanted to Go." *Classic Toy Trains* (February 1992).

CARP, ROGER. "The Magic of Bob James' American Flyer Window Displays." *Classic Toy Trains* (November 1993).

DE VAULT, DAVID W. "The World's Longest Santa Claus Parade." *Trains* (December 1986).

DOLZALL, GARY. "Shadows of Things That Have Been." *Trains* (December 1982).

FRANCIK, WILLIAM B., JR. "Working Amtrak's California Zephyr." *Trains* (December 1989).

GARVEY, MICHAEL. As told to Swearingen, John A. "The Sharing of a Caring Stranger." *Trains* (December 1999).

GOHMANN, JOHN W. "Christmas on the Cities." *Trains* (December 2000).

HENSLER, HAL. "The Gift of a Lifetime." *Classic Toy Trains* (December 1998).

HOUSER, FRED N. "Wartime Fan Trip." Classic *Trains* (Winter 2001).

HUSTER, JOHN. "Toy Trains and Christmas Memories." *Trains* (November 1993).

JACOBS, JOHN C. As told to Swearingen, John A. "The Ghost of a Christmas Present." *Trains* (December 1998).

JESENSKY, JOE. "The Christmas Gift That Kept Giving." *Classic Toy Trains* (December 1995).

KATZ, CURTIS L. "The Gift." *Classic Trains* (Winter 2001).

KEIRCE, BILL. "Buddy 'L' for Christmas." *Classic Toy Trains* (December 1995).

MCCORMICK, AMOS. "A Slice of History." *Classic Toy Trains* (November 1993).

MCDONNELL, GREG J. "Montreal for Christmas," *Trains* (December 1986)

RALSTON, ROBERT O. "Holiday Homecoming." *Trains* (December 2002).

RUNG, AL. "Christmas Eve on the Broadway." *Trains* (December 1948).

SEVY, NORMAN L. "Christmas on a Caboose." *Trains* (December 1986).

SNORTELAND, BILL. "Holiday Spirit on the Pennsy." *Trains* (December 1993).

STAAB, J. THOMAS. "Christmas Dinner on the GN." *Trains* (December 1998).

STRINGFELLOW, JAMIE. "Into the Valley of Believers." *Yankee Magazine* (December 1998).

WELLS, FLOYD. "Christmas Train." *Trains* (December 1998).

WITHERS, BOB. "A Passenger Palace." *Classic Trains* (Fall 2000).

————— ."West Virginia Winter Odyssey." *Trains* (December 1996).

ZIRUL, ARTHUR. "Arthur Godfrey's Christmas Bargain." *Classic Toy Trains* (December 1995).

ZOLLO, JOHN. "A Macy's Mistake." *Classic Toy Trains* (December 1995).

CREDITS